The Future-Focused Organization

The Future-Focused Organization

Complete Organizational Alignment For Breakthrough Results

Terence T. Burton
and
John W. Moran

Prentice Hall PTR
Englewood Cliffs, New Jersey 07632

Library of Congress Cataloging-in-Publication Data

Burton, Terence T.
 The future-focused organization : complete organizational
 alignment for breakthrough results / by Terence T. Burton, John
 W. Moran.
   p. cm,
 Includes index.
 ISBN 0-13-323791-5
 1. Organizational effectiveness. 2. Strategic planning.
I. Moran, John W. II. Title.
HD58.9.M67 1995   94-39008
658.4'012—dc20   CIP

Editorial/production supervision: *BooksCraft, Inc. Indianapolis, IN*
Cover design: *Sue Behnke*
Cover photo: *H. / O. Peitgen, H. Jürgens, and D. Saupe*
Manufacturing manager: *Alexis R. Heydt*
Acquisitions editor: *Bernard Goodwin*

©1995 Prentice Hall PTR
Prentice-Hall, Inc.
A Simon & Schuster Company
Englewood Cliffs, New Jersey 07632

The publisher offers discounts on this book when ordered
in bulk quantities. For more information, contact:

  Corporate Sales Department
  Prentice Hall PTR
  113 Sylvan Avenue
  Englewood Cliffs, NJ 07632

  Phone: 800-382-3419 or 201-592-2498
  Fax: 201-592-2249
  email: dan_rush@prenhall.com

Printed in the United States of America
10 9 8 7 6 5 4 3 2 1

ISBN: 0-13-323791-5

Prentice-Hall International (UK) Limited, *London*
Prentice-Hall of Australia Pty. Limited, *Sydney*
Prentice-Hall Canada Inc., *Toronto*
Prentice-Hall Hispanoamericana, S.A., *Mexico*
Prentice-Hall of India Private Limited, *New Delhi*
Prentice-Hall of Japan, Inc., *Tokyo*
Simon & Schuster Asia Pte. Ltd., *Singapore*
Editora Prentice-Hall do Brasil, Ltda., *Rio de Janeiro*

Contents

Foreword vii

Preface xxi

1 The Future-Focused Organization 1

2 Involving the Total Organization 13

3 Future-Focused Organization Structure 29

4 The Omni Pattern 57

5 Competitive Analysis 83

6 Future-Focused Organization Planning
  Process 101

7 Focusing and Expanding Customer
  Expectations... 131

8   The Virtual Super Team................................ 143

9   The Hiring, Growing, and Rewarding
    Process 179

10 Charting and Staying the Course 193

11 Summary.. 207

    Index.. 215

Foreword

This is an exciting time for American industry. During the last decade, many organizations have implemented a variety of tactical continuous improvement programs to increase competitiveness. A partial list of these programs at our company has included MRP II, JIT, TQM & SPC, EDI, CIM, DFX, TPM, Downsizing, and Employee Involvement Teams. These activities have helped us through the 1980s and have built a solid foundation for future change. However, despite our collective progress, American industry still has a long road ahead to recapture its dominant position in the world economy. The good news is that many executives recognize this fact and are serious about rewriting the fundamental rules of industrial order in their companies.

Galileo Electro-Optics Corporation develops, manufactures, and markets fiber-optic and electro-optic components, assemblies and systems that sense, transmit, or intensify light and images or detect and multiply electrons, charged particles, and electromagnetic radiation. Three years ago, military business represented over 85% of the company's sales, primarily in very intricate and expensive night-vision components. Today, commercial business represents over 90% of our sales, and we do not have the luxury of selling $10,000 night-vision systems to consumers. Our defense conversion was achieved by developing totally new products based on our core technologies and competencies. As a result, we serve new markets, which include office products, analytical instrumentation, medical visualization and research, display image processing, process analysis, space science and research, and development laboratories. We at Galileo recognized that the velocity and magnitude of change required to support a successful commercial transition exceeded our continuous improvement efforts and that focusing on the "as is" was just not enough to make a difference in the global marketplace.

The need for breakthrough change in our company is shared by many organizations. Whether it is defense conversion, improving profitability, or managing high growth, the need to manage change, change, and more change is inevitable. Recognition of this need was the result of passing through that uncomfortable stage when the organization's ideas no longer work, and that is so uncomfortable that the natural reaction is to either ignore it, postpone dealing with it, or retreat from it. We did none of these, but instead locked our employees in this stage with us, making them confront change, uncertainty, chaos, survival, and confusion together. We set out to invent new breakthroughs in business performance through a total reengineering of our entire company. We challenged our own strategies and conventions, assumed the larger risks of throwing away outdated practices and starting over, and began to pursue fundamental, structural changes in the way we operated our company. We made a significant investment in our employees, equipping them with new skills to reengineer and manage breakthrough change, to think together and benefit from change, rather than become victims of change. To some onlookers, our transformation might have appeared impossible, unthinkable, ridiculous, or incredibly aggressive. To our employees it has been both difficult and challenging, and, believe me, it is much more difficult in practice than it looks in the *Harvard Business Review* or *Business Week*.

Reengineering is rapidly becoming a way of life in our organization, as natural as taking a deep breath. Reinventing new rules of industrial order at Galileo has involved the full empowerment of employees to question our deep-rooted strategic, technological, and structural purposes for existence. We also learned that business process redesign and changing the fundamental ways that work gets done required a different organizational model, *a future-focused organization*. The conventional approaches of reshuffling and shifting boxes on the organization chart were no longer practical to support our reengineering efforts. We needed to invent a new model that could function like a kaleidoscope—extremely disciplined, structured, and focused but adjustable with a simple movement. The characteristics of this new model include flatness, agility, seamlessness or boundarylessness, virtual and instantaneously correcting to customer needs, and elimination of functional and hierarchical boundaries. Our future-focused organization has transformed a homogeneous, functional structure into self-managing and self-adjusting business teams focused on critical customers and markets. These teams are empowered to operate as independent, de facto small businesses within the overall business.

The future-focused organization in our company has been both a destination and a journey. It is a destination because we arrived at this new model only after we successfully reengineered the entire company. The complete reinvention, repositioning, restructuring, and rebuilding of our business has made this new organization possible. Anyone who reads this book and thinks that they can implement their own future-focused organization by next Monday is sadly mistaken. Our version of the future-focused organization is also a journey because, as we strive to reengineer our business to perfection, we continue to advance the structure and dynamics of this model and how we use it.

It is funny how things happen in life. As our future-focused organization evolved, we began to observe that it had characteristics similar to fractal science—one of the core technologies of our company. For example, refer to the Mandelbrot fractal in Figure F.1. This graphic appears to be an unstructured, random, and confusing geometric pattern. However, its construction is a well-defined order that evolves from a specific point via a mathematical formula. A future-focused organization may also appear confusing; however, its composition is also a well-defined set of flexible processes and individuals that is assembled on demand to support specific customer needs. A future-focused organization can be flexed and reshaped as easily as modifying the parameters of the formula, which would alter the geometric pattern of our Mandelbrot set.

Looking back, we accepted this process of chaos because chaos is the root of our technology. As glass and ceramics engineers, we appreciate the notion of chaos and recognize that the natural order of a fractal system changes only when it is forced off the balance of equilibrium. That is exactly what we did with our organizational model. We forced ourselves out of equilibrium and accepted the challenges of reengineering, reinvention, and chaos. Two of our employees wrote an article about our future-focused organization model, comparing its behavior to

Figure F.1 A Mathematical Arrangement of Thousands of These Points Magnified

that of our fused fiber-optic technology, and the new order became crystal clear to everyone! Using this fractal thinking, we accepted chaos and moving out of our comfort zones.

Fundamentally Fractal

Of convoluted curves and transcendent teams.

By: Susan M. Patterson
   Manager of Fiber Array Development
   Danna A. Mancini
   Product Development Engineer
   Galileo Electro-Optics Corporation
   Sturbridge, Massachusetts

I : Fractal Overview

Using our minds and the power of rational thought, people have been endeavoring for centuries to understand the natural world that surrounds us. Scholars would examine the evidence and put forth theories, rules and "laws of nature" which would then be modified as needed to accommodate newly discovered evidence. Unfortunately, from time to time, a phenomenon is revealed which is obviously contrary to the currently accepted explanation. At this point, one of two courses of action is taken. First, the accepted interpretation of reality is substantially revised to include the latest information. Second, try as we might, a new understanding, which could include the disrupting revelation, succeeds in eluding us and the matter is tossed into a collection of "curiosities" and then forgotten.

In the field of mathematics, many of these curiosities pertain to graphed equations whose "curve" have no unique point of tangency. Early experimenters commonly referred to them as "monsters" or being "grotesque." Later, with the arrival of analytical geometry, such graphs came to be described as "pathological," "nonlinear" and "irrational." Less than twenty years ago, in 1975, Benoit B. Mandelbrot christened this new field of study "Fractal Geometry." Today, those same chaotic orphans of mathematics are considered to be creations of rare and extreme "beauty," thanks to Mandelbrot and color computer imaging (see Figure F.2).

Multiple iterations and self-symmetry are the two most distinguishing features of fractal curves. Passing the data repeatedly through the formula (multiple iterations) with the use of a computer creates an infinitely complex image. Any area in that image can then be zoomed in on and, eventually, the original image will reappear.

The graph of a fractal curve at any particular scale also has multiple areas where the geometric shapes will be almost identical (self-symmetry) except for size and orientation. These fea-

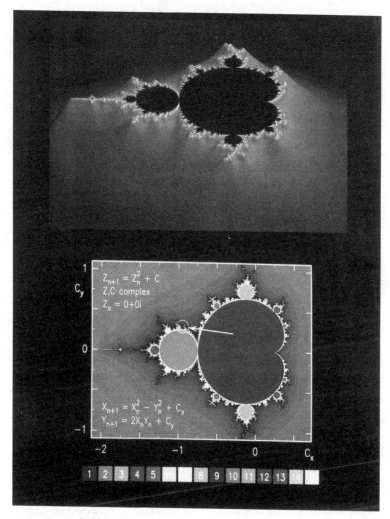

Figure F.2   Computer-generated Fractal Image

tures are the tools that we have used at Galileo to develop a new and superior breed of fiber optics.

II: Technical Application

The standard building block of fused fiber-optics at Galileo for many years has been the 61-piece hexagon (Figure F.3). Present-day applications of this long-standing technology to new products are based on trial and error, with a bit of myth and legend mixed in. The main problem with this geometrical format is that the relatively flat sides do not interlock (Figure F.4), allowing dislocation of individual fibers within larger arrays. This fiber movement produces unwanted disorder and image distortion in the final fiber-optic product. In order to achieve any semblance of order at all, these fibers must be kept in line through the use of clamps and molds which provide the much needed external constraining forces.

In 1989 several of us at Galileo decided that it was time to reengineer the basic building block of our core technology through the application of modern scientific analysis. Using basic fractal geometry, we developed the 49-piece cluster shown in Figure F.5. The beauty of the 49-piece fractal fiber is

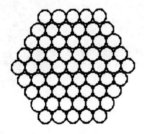

Figure F.3   61-piece Hexagon

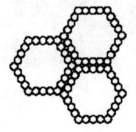

Figure F.4   Noninterlocking Fibers

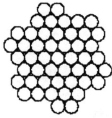
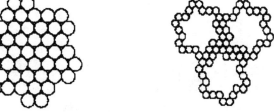

Figure F.5   49-piece Cluster   **Figure F.6**   Iterative Tilting

its corrugated perimeter which provides interlocking and self-referencing when assembled into large arrays. Fractal architecture intrinsically requires substantially less external force to maintain a near perfect hexagonal array. These fibers, through the application of iterative tiling (Figure F.6), can also provide the means for the theoretically unlimited scaling of arrays. Thus, the finished product has no distortion, and no distortion means improved optical performance and efficiency.

III: Organizational Application

Just as fractal theory has been a very useful tool for resolving complex problems in the scientific world, the same basic principles can also be applied to create very efficient organizations. The traditional organization, for example, has similar flaws as compared to the traditional fiber optic described above. Its structure (Figure F.7) is defined by the multilayered organization chart that is based on a hierarchy of simple, segregated departments, each of which performs a specifically defined function. The boundaries between functional departments are present and very rigid, even with employee involvement and teaming activities of the past. The "orders" are typically initiated from an external vantage point called "management," and the "workers" mindlessly perform the tasks, providing little, if

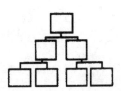

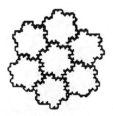

Figure F.7   Traditional Organization

Figure F.8   Interlocking, Self-management Teams

any, feedback. This scenario restricts efficiency and communication, limiting the overall productivity and success of the organization on the whole.

In an effort to maximize the performance of any organization, one might reengineer the traditional organization by transforming its structure from one that is department or problem oriented into one made up of holistic self-managed teams. These new self-managed teams can be thought of as the interlocking (Figure F.8), self-referencing building blocks described in fractal theory. Each team, requiring very little external guidance to function, would be created to act on measurable objectives that would contribute to the overall success of the organization. The team approach is a way of tapping into the dormant resources that are available, encouraging every employee to use their mind and take on ownership of their work. This goes beyond the traditional thinking of team-based problem solving and encourages the use of standalone business teams as the new structure of the total organization. Future organizations would essentially be virtual networks of these self-managed, interactive, ever changing teams; stretching known limits, knocking down barriers that surround them, and accomplishing things that have never been achieved before.

Fractal geometry, more than traditional Euclidean geometry, accurately describes how objects in nature are constructed and appear. By applying fractal concepts to our creations and to our organizations, we can all reap the profits and benefits of simplicity, order, flexibility and efficiency.

Chaos in fractal geometry, in business, in nature, and in life is created by simple structured events. Chaos is nothing more than unpredictable order with some limits, and chaos remains chaos unless it is followed by actions that define order. In business, managing chaos effectively means recognizing and satisfying a multitude of customer needs, self-managing, self-adjusting, and shifting resources at the speed of sound. From the outside, this organizational model might appear fragmented and confusing, with very unclear lines of authority and garbled functions. However, the reality is that a future-focused organization is a collage of extremely focused, disciplined, and structured business teams that have learned how to instantaneously adjust to new customer and market needs.

Unfortunately, chaos, fear, and threat are synonymous to many managers and that is a severe shortfall in U.S. industry. Chaos demands an appreciation of natural order and how it is created. When magnified, chaos is always underlined by a structured, repeating order. For example, a seacoast looks just as complex at 5000 feet as it does when magnified, but the structure is grains of sand and molecules of water interlocked by the order of the elements. When we walk on the sand, this natural system appears loose and unstructured; however, it is very disciplined and uses the capacity for self-reference to adjust and preserve itself. The sand and the water are focused on what they are, recognizing that the process may change but they will never lose their core integrity. There are no managers making sure that the molecules of sand hold on to each other or that the molecules of water flow in such a way as to level the sand. It just happens naturally at the lowest elements in the process, and this is the same phenomenon we are creating in the future-focused organization. This is not the total elimination of functional management because, like the seacoast, someone must maintain the dunes, monitor land use and environmental conditions, or reengineer the system by building sea walls or breakwater structures. The future-focused organization is a hybrid structure leaning heavily in the direction of self-management of critical customer processes, virtual teamwork, and individual autonomy.

For centuries, we have designed organizations as if they were machines. Machines have separate parts designed with different functions and tolerances. The machine is designed for a specific purpose, and broken or worn parts are easily replaceable. There is no room for chaos and significant variability in purpose. The future-focused organization is analogous to designing a machine that can make anything with a few fast maintenance adjustments. The new order of business is anticipating real market opportunities and designing how execution processes and structures are linked together to create stakeholder success. The purpose, the goals, and the core competencies may remain more stable, but the processes and structures by which we satisfy customer needs must constantly change. Organizations that are committed to managing chaos and the constant reengineering of themselves for agility, seamlessness, and responsiveness will become the emerging industrial corporations of the 21st century. Organizations that prefer equilibrium and business as usual will either fail outright or become, in effect, local design, marketing, or manufacturing subsidiaries of their global competitors.

The authors present radical ideas about organizational structures and processes in *The Future-Focused Organization*. When I read this book, I liked it because many of the concepts were living images of the organizational model we have implemented at Galileo. We are an evolving, living sandbox that demonstrates that the principles work well and provide solid underpinnings for breakthrough improvement. *The Future-Focused Organization* provides both vision and implementation approaches for organizations of the future. Success requires going beyond reading this book, accepting revolutionary change as the norm, and remembering that the risks of equilibrium are much more dangerous than the risks of positively managed chaos.

William T. Hanley
President and Chief Executive Officer
Galileo Electro-Optics Corporation
Sturbridge, Massachusetts

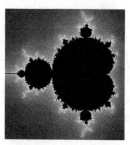

Preface

Let's reflect on the evolution of organizational models in corporate America. We have witnessed various trends of centralized versus decentralized, structured versus unstructured, functional verses team based, matrix management, delayered flat structures, roulette wheel structures, top-down and bottom-up, formal versus informal, and probably many other approaches to managing organizations. Today, management is not sure when it should plan, control, delegate, empower, intervene, or create another team to solve the company's problems. One executive commented recently, "We used to have functional silos. Now we have a whole barnyard of programs and teams, and to be honest I've lost track of what they're all doing." As a result, many executives are struggling with how to continue this evolution of repositioning their organizations to compete globally in the 21st century.

The focus of this book is on helping an organization and its leadership to develop a future-focused strategic business development and deployment process. This book answers the question of how the organization should rapidly adjust and redeploy resources so that it will always be in the leadership position in its marketplace. We refer to this model as the *future-focused organization*. This organization provides the underpinnings of success by bringing the terms agile, fluid, or seamless to life through people. This new model is also a must for those organizations pursuing revolutionary change through reengineering or seeking the next level of excellence in their total quality management, cycle time reduction, or other continuous improvement efforts.

This future-focused strategic business process is a radical change from the widely practiced and popular POSDCER process of plan, organize, staff, delegate, check, execute, and then replan. The future-focused strategic business process outlined in this book puts the executive team in the "do" loop by specifying their duties on how to deploy the plan so that it is achieved in the most timely and efficient manner for the organization. The planning and deployment of corporate strategic direction must have a cycle time measure. The future-focused strategic business process utilizes the organizational resources effectively and efficiently. The planning and deployment of business strategy must not be a valueless and disruptive yearly event to the organization. In many organizations that we have worked with the strategic business planning and deployment process is dreaded because it is an event-based process. The output of the event is a document that is bookshelf bound and not results bound. Planning and deployment must be a real-time process, performed by 100% of the work force. Stated another way, organizational agility and adjustment must become a people-driven process that is as natural as breathing.

This future-focused strategic business process helps the organization to know what to change, how to cause the change in the most efficient and painless manner, and how to time and cause the change to happen. From this process the organization will know what is important, what is a strength, what has value, and what does not. It will know when an approach has been useful and when to discard it. It will know when a business process contributes to customer success or when to reengineer it away. Its strategic business strategies will deal more with cultural change factors than traditional operational and financial factors. This process will allow the organization to be the "best practices industry benchmark." The organization transforms itself from supervision to creative leadership, and will learn to develop a reliance on and trust in those in the cross-functional lateral and functional daily management positions since they have the fundamental understanding of the business. Creative leadership will focus on the panoramic future of the organization and lead by macromanagement, not by the traditional micromanagement.

Creative leadership will master the fine art of virtual partnerships that are interorganizational and external to the organization in order to maximize the leveraging of their scarce resources.

The leadership will expend their scarce resources to change how they service their customer base now and in the future, rather than on public relations to change their image. Their image will be changed by their long-term actions.

An organization that follows this future-focused process will not be trying to duplicate its past glory days[1], or to rejuvenate or reinvent itself.[2] It will be causing its competition to do this since it will be the market pace setter for all others to imitate.

1. Can Xerox Duplicate Its Glory Days?, *Business Week*, October 4, 1993, No. 3339, pp. 56–58.
2. Why Mercedes Is Alabama Bound, *Business Week*, October 11, 1993, No. 3340, pp. 138–39.

Such organizations are future focused in all their actions. To achieve this, there must be common commitment at the top and alignment and partnerships throughout the rest of the organization to achieve future-focused goals and objectives.

A future-focused organization is lead by individuals who are up to the challenge to take charge of their organization and lead it to its destiny. Few leaders today are prepared for this challenge. Instead, we read many articles that point out that a CEO seemed to be caught off guard when sales waned, or profits dropped, or technology past his organization by, and so on.[3]

Our unemployment figures reflect the inability of managers to maintain a future-focused view for their organizations. Our corporate landscape is littered with the shells of former great organizations whose leaders did not have the vision to see their organization's future unraveling before them. A ride around Route 128 in Massachusetts or through Silicon Valley, Detroit, Cleveland, or Bethlehem brings this reality home. Unfortunately, when reality struck, such organizations were ill equipped to deal with the problems and unable to respond quickly to offset their devastating effects.

Some of these former great organizations of the 1980s have either ceased to exist, are 50% to 75% of their previous selves, or have merged for survival and lost their identity. One such organization that the future overtook no longer trades on the stock exchange and at its pinnacle had 37,000 employees.

In addition to the organization's demise or downsizing, other spillover effects of managers' inability to keep a future-focused view include the following:

---

3. Has Syntex Run Out of Steam?, *Business Week*, July 12, 1993, pp. 144–146.

- High unemployment (1.2 million jobs in manufacturing lost since 1989; this equals 6% of the work force)
- Family unit disruption and destruction
- Individual financial devastation
- Local economic ruin

This is a high price for society as a whole to pay for managers of these former great giants not maintaining a future-focused view.

During the last decade, enormous energy, expenses, and capital investment have been expended in the elusive search for answers to improve industry competitiveness. Many organizations have become paralyzed by their belief that continuous improvement must be slow and steady, but tortoises only win races in fairy tales. And benchmarking has taught us that being the best tortoise in the group is not all that impressive to the 1990s customer.

The purpose of this book is to get executives to recognize that despite our progress, U.S. industry is still replete with implicit organizational rules left over from earlier decades. Companies must now shift paradigms, move boundaries, change the rules, and redefine the templates and fundamental assumptions about how they manage their business.

This book focuses on helping senior managers develop an attitude that goes beyond day-to-day continuous improvement of the organization's current functions. It explains how, and it leads senior management to adopt a view that is focused on the future, that is, the next 5 to 10 years. The book shows senior management how they must constantly monitor their environment if they wish to keep their competitive edge and market leadership position.

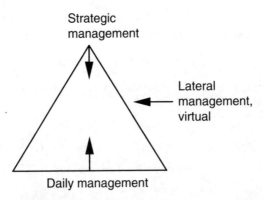

Figure P.1   Types of Future-focused Management

This book stresses that to be a future-focused organization requires a permanent and fluid or virtual organization structure composed of three types of management: strategic management, lateral management, and daily management (see Fig. P.1). Lateral management is the fluid or virtual structure in the organization. The other two types of structure are permanent parts of the organization.

This book shows senior management how to plan and involve the organization to focus, redefine, and expand customer expectations. In addition, a number of tools are included to help the reader accomplish this.

The future-focused organization is an alternative approach to the *doomsday or crisis management* style being popularized today in much business writings and many seminars. This future-focused organization book details a process that can accomplish a radical transformation of an organization in a positive and proactive manner, rather than in a negative and reactionary manner, thereby maintaining the company's integrity and employee satisfaction.

The leaders of future-focused organizations do not wait for nor create crises to motivate organizations to change radically.

These leaders keep their organizations focused, lean, and able to quickly react to any change or opportunity in the marketplace. These future-focused organization leaders see a crisis forming far on the horizon, view it as an opportunity, and focus the organization well in advance not only to meet the crisis head on but to prepare to emerge from the crisis with an enhanced competitive advantage.

Future-focused organization leaders do not allow themselves to be imprisoned in the past or languish in the present, but instead they focus on how they should be operating to remain the market leader and provider of choice. They recognize the belief systems and convictions that inhibit breakthrough improvement and full employee stewardship. They have brought the seamless, business team organization to life by empowering employees to execute and benefit from change, rather than become victims of competitor's changes.

The future-focused organization approach details a path for an organization to follow that results in a crisis in their competitor's organization but not their own. The future-focused organization is always focusing on change to maintain its leadership position and no longer considers change just when a real or manufactured crisis appears.

A future-focused organization is always making change, but in a controlled and focused way that constantly increases its strategic advantage portfolio in the marketplace. Future-focused organizations are controlled and focused revolutions that constantly hunt down and eliminate the rebels of arrogance, overconfidence, status quo maintainers, and nonreality acceptors.

Doomsday or crisis management accomplishes short-term change but does long-term damage to the organization's infrastructure. Short-term radical change raises havoc within an organization by producing winners and losers. A future-focused organization approach has a win–win result for the organization and its employees.

This book is written for senior executives, strategic planners, market and sales managers, and designers of current or emerging organizations. It is for all types of organizations—manufacturing, service, health care, government, education, and so on.

The Future-Focused Organization goes a step beyond current management materials and focuses on the organization's need to develop loyal customers and employees. The future-focused organization places an emphasis on the need to have constant, well-planned revolutions that restructure the organization and focus it on the future through a self-help approach. It is the approach that will take organizations into the 21st century.

Acknowledgments

The authors would like to acknowledge the following individuals for their help, guidance, useful comments, and constructive criticisms. We are indebted to them for trying the concepts presented in this book, as well as their dedication in helping us to meet our many deadlines. We truly value their friendship and encouragement.

- Roger Berger
  Professor
  Iowa State University
  Department of Industrial Management and Systems Engineering

- Fred A. Caterino
  Director
  Tambrands, Inc.

- Charlie Chapman
  Executive Vice-president
  President, North America
  Tambrands, Inc.

- Joann DeMott
  President
  The J. DeMott Company

- William T. Hanley
  President and Chief Executive Officer
  Galileo Electro-Optics Corporation

- Glen Hoffherr
  Founding Principal
  Strategic Total Enterprise Management Institute

- John Hoffman
  President
  John Hoffman and Associates

- Tom Kuras
  New Hampshire Technical Colleges and Institute
  Director, TQM Programs

- Michael Marcos
  Royal Bank of Canada
  Manager, Strategic Planning
  Retail Banking

- Marilyn McIntosh
  Keebler Company
  Training Facilitator
  Agent for Cultural Change

- Suzette Rielly
  Polaroid Corporation
  Education and Training Associate

The Future-Focused Organization

A *future-focused organization* is one that clearly understands its three most important attributes, the *past, present,* and *future.*

The past provides the foundation for growth. The past focused the organization on its purpose. The purpose[1] of an organization is defined as

- Its mission, primary concern, goal, or objective
- Having precision and clarity
- Being specific but not limiting

Every word added to the purpose statement reduces the solution space. Modifiers are restrictive. Modifiers are the words the corporate song writers add to the purpose statement to save their entrenched positions and power. These added modifiers transform the purpose into a useless, unachievable vision.

---

1. G. Hoffherr, J. Moran, and G. Nadler, *Breakthrough Thinking in Total Quality Management,* Prentice Hall PTR, Englewood Cliffs, N.J., 1994.

1

This early on focus on purpose is critical for an organization to be competitive, a viable force in the marketplace, and successful for the long-term. This early focus on purpose should drive the organization to define and build its needed core competencies. Core competencies will define the needed critical systems and critical processes[2] to accomplish the purpose. The purpose needs to be reviewed on a regular basis to keep the organization fresh and focused on its customers and their changing needs and culture.

Such future-focused organizations do not hang on to a dying business segment but instead spin off and invest in the next higher purpose. Future-focused organizations are constantly changing and sharpening their focus on their purpose.

The present develops the foundation for the future. We need to project into the future to determine what the shifting corporate landscape might look like 2 to 5 years in the future. We need to answer the following questions:

- What will the marketplace landscape look like?
- Who will be our biggest competitor?
- How big a lead in the marketplace will they have over us?
- What strengths will we be able to offer our customers?
- Will our culture support the changes that may be needed?
- Do we have the appropriate core competencies?
- Can we anticipate and change our culture to meet the demands of our purpose?
- And so on.

---

2. C. Collett, J. DeMott, and J. Moran, *Introduction to Critical Process,* a GOAL/ QPC Application Report, No. 92-01A, GOAL/QPC, Methuen, Mass., 1992.

The present is a step in the revitalization of an organization. In the present we refocus on our core competencies (critical systems and critical processes) and develop the strategic plan based on the purpose we want to achieve in the next 3 to 5 years. We do not develop strategy based on the ambition of the leaders or our existing resources. We develop strategy to achieve our purpose and to delight our customers and not ourselves.

In the present stage we develop the purpose hierarchy for our organization and the cultural hierarchy as shown in Figure 1.1. Once the organization understands the purpose it has to achieve and the location of its culture, it can see where the disconnects may be. One common outcome of this exercise is that the organization understands that its current culture does not support the attainment of its purpose and that change, sometimes radical change, is needed.

If the organization depicted in Figure 1.1 tries to move from the today position on the purpose hierarchy to the 3-year position without making a similar move in its cultural hierarchy, it will introduce a tremendous stress factor into the organization. This stress factor slows down the rate of change since the individuals involved do not feel competent to now make starters because it requires a different skill set. Organizations must learn to make purpose shifts with the appropriate cultural shifts simultaneously. Both the purpose shift and the cultural shift require an investment. The investment in the purpose shift is largely in terms of capital. The investment in the cultural shift is mainly in human terms: supporting, training, understanding, listening, involving, communicating, and guiding the employees to the new purpose. Unfortunately the cultural investment is usually poorly made and does not reap the dividends it should. Cultural investment is never smooth

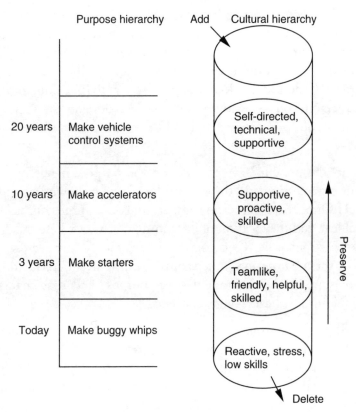

Figure 1.1   Future-Focused Organizations Hierarchies

but rather chaotic, cyclical, with many starts, stops, and restarts and much confusion. The same care that goes into developing a capital investment should be made for a cultural investment.

Both authors once worked for an organization whose purpose change was not made through careful planning, but by a very quick shift in the technology available to the marketplace. It had to play catch-up in a hurry. The engineering staff was trained in one discipline, but an entirely new discipline was required. The organization's leadership decided to retrain the engineering staff in the new discipline. This caused tremendous stress since it was done in an atmosphere of sink or swim. Some engineers had not been in a formal learning setting for years and were threatened by the prospect of going to class and being graded (management would see all grades and make them part of the next performance rating), and others never went to school but learned on the job and were petrified of a classroom setting. No support was given to those being retrained; some left, some were demoted, some survived, and many new people were hired, and much resentment still remains today. A little time and energy spent on the cultural investment would have made the transition easier for those involved and the purpose change happen more quickly.

The organization must also check its organization's purpose and culture against its customer culture as shown in Figure 1.2. Future-focused organizations must check and monitor to see that shifts are detected and reacted to quickly. These customer cultural shifts will have a dramatic impact on the market.

An example of changing customer culture and its impact on an organization's purpose is the recent announcement by a company in the home canning supply business that it was spinning off its core business to focus on the manufacturing and marketing of glass and metal containers for large food processors. Its home canning customer's culture had changed. The change was from family values to convenience. The family values had shifted from the traditional stay-at-home family who gardened and preserved food to a culture of "when we need food we go to the supermarket." This is a case where the organization was at a lower level in its purpose and cultural hierarchy and its customer was at a much higher one. Being able to

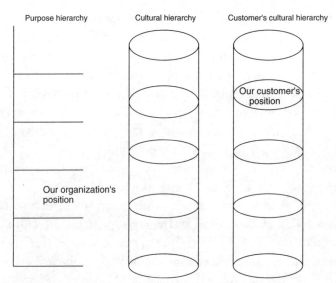

Figure 1.2   Future-Focused Organizations Hierarchies

identify these imbalances in hierarchy levels between an organization and its customers helps an organization position or change its product or service before it becomes obsolete.

In the present we must begin to project to the future to determine the following:

- ✏ Current competitors' potential movements and their impacts on the marketplace.

- ✏ Customer's changing culture and its impact on the marketplace and organization.

- ✏ Potential new entrants into the marketplace and the change they may cause.

- ✏ Potential new technology and its impact.

- ✏ Our ability to influence and redefine customer expectations.

☞ The appropriate product bundles to invest in and develop.

The future is where a future-focused organization's fortune and continued existence lie and it must be discovered. The future-focused organization is constantly on a discovery and focusing journey. There is a portion of every part of the future-focused organization's that is focused on discovering new opportunities, technologies, combinations, product bundles, potentials, and so on. Discovery is one part of the process; blending discovery with purpose is the other part.

Many organizations are currently suffering from the bad economy syndrome, which stems from a corporate mentality of "get an order for anything that we can build, from anyone who is willing to do business with us." This mission typically leads organizations to become unfocused as they attempt desperately to service hundreds of customers with thousands of product configurations. They also unconsciously allow themselves to become distracted from the markets and strategic customers that provide the largest future potential and whose requirements are better aligned with the company's core competencies. The bad economy syndrome is shown in Figure 1.3.

A reengineering process called *mission, vision, purpose* (MVP) *filtering* is a formal process that is used to reposition and refocus organizations for competitive advantage.[3] This process reconciles "fits" and "gaps" between potential customer or market requirements and a company's core competencies. Customers and markets are slotted into operational business units, or OBUs, based on core competency mapping, and these categories are the basis for reengineering the company. Operational

---

3. T. Burton, J. Moran, and M. Fitipiak, *The Reengineering Toolbox*, The Center for Excellence in Operations, Inc., 1994, pp. 1–11.

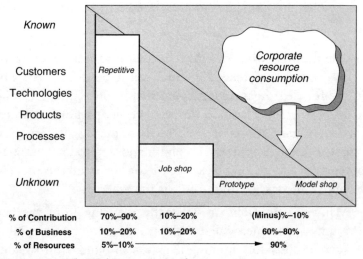

Figure 1.3 The Bad Economy Syndrome

business units are defined according to the predictability of customers, technologies, products, and processes. At one end of
the spectrum is a repetitive OBU (for example, a group of customers with repeat business or large customers that have placed
larger blanket orders for standard products over a fixed time
horizon). At the other end of the spectrum are prototype and
model shop OBUs (for example, customers with small, unique,
and undefined needs). The result is self-contained business
teams (for example, 8 to 16 cross-functional employees
equipped with the full scope of business skills) that operate
autonomously as de facto small businesses and service the full
needs of their customer operational business unit from design
to delivery. This is a radical departure from tradition: strong,
well-defined reporting relationships to customers; employees in
constant contact with customers about design, quality, or proposed continuous improvements; OBUs and customer work
cells that are responsible for all aspects of their business (not

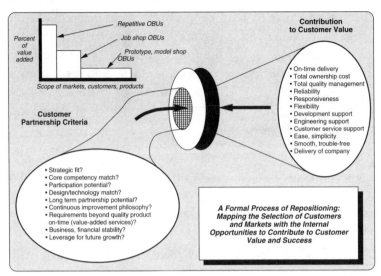

Figure 1.4 MVP Filtering

just quality); and a flat, fluid boundaryless organization that is capable of adjusting instantaneously. Mission, vision, purpose filtering is shown in Figure 1.4.

For example, one client selected a small group of approximately 25 customers and focused the company's total capabilities. These customers generated 90% of the company's revenues, and their requirements matched the organization's core competencies perfectly. The only problem with this new approach was that in the beginning revenues fell as some customers were turned away. Soon the company unclogged its quotation and engineering departments and purged its manufacturing facilities and was much better positioned to improve the services of their key accounts.

Through reengineering, this client moved from an "all things to all people" strategy to a niche strategy closely aligned to their technical, business, market, and service strengths.

They refocused their marketing efforts with an emphasis on longer-term, value-added partnerships, and new accounts are put through their MVP filtering litmus test. The company now provides value-added design, products, and services to a smaller base of true, customer partnerships. And today they are growing and hiring employees while 100% of their local competitors are downsizing!

In summary:

Future-focused organizations do not dream up visions based on their current capabilities and then expend enormous resources to accomplish them. They focus on capability-driven purpose.

Future-focused organizations focus their resources on the purpose.

Future-focused organizations have a culture in which change is expected and learning is continuous.

Future-focused organizations recognize their existing core competencies and deploy them in ways that maximize customer success. They also anticipate future market needs and acquire the core competencies necessary to succeed in these new opportunities.

Future-focused organizations are constantly changing, sometimes incrementally and sometimes radically, to fulfill competency-based purpose requirements.

Future-focused organizations' current and potential customers are delighted and not just satisfied from this process of achieving competency-based purpose. This delight comes from the alignment of the organization with the customer's culture.

Future-focused organizations ensure that all parties, internally and externally, are having their needs met profitably.

Future-focused organizations have decision-making and prioritization processes that are clear, transparent, and at the point of need.

Future-focused organizations develop employees who understand what they need to do to satisfy their internal and external customers. They are also willing and able to change as it is needed. The appropriate support and training are provided to make the change go smoothly. Then employees have a willingness and desire to speak up, which is matched by management's desire to listen.

Future-focused organizations understand that they need a constant blending of capital and knowledge to survive. Capital and knowledge are the ingredients, when blended correctly, that produce the product and service bundles that customers want and value.

Future-focused organizations make the appropriate short-term investments to ensure that this process of change and continuous learning is achieved in the long term.

Future-focused organizations do not jump from one management technique to the next. They do not adopt total quality management this year, then reengineer the next year, only to settle for the next six months on a process to develop the appropriate organizational architecture,[4] and so on.

Future-focused organizations do not overlook the new and emerging business thinkers. A future-focused organization listens, extracts, and adapts those elements from the new business thinkers that provide new building blocks that support and expand its purpose hierarchy. The people in a future-focused organization do not view this adaptation to new thought as a change in direction or another program of the

---

4. Management's New Gurus, *Business Week*, August 31, 1992, pp. 44–52.

month. They view it as continuous learning to help them focus and accomplish the change needed to survive and be a market leader and not a market reactor.

Future-focused organizations do not sacrifice tomorrow on the altar of yesterday. Future-focused organizations do not sacrifice activities aimed at building a different tomorrow to keep yesterday alive a little longer.[5]

In summary, a future-focused organization is constantly focused on learning and adapting to run the organization so that the right things get done routinely, the customer's needs are met and anticipated, the purpose is in focus and is refined regularly, and the company and its employees grow financially.

---

5. Peter F. Drucker, Drucker on Management, *Wall Street Journal*, February 2, 1993, p. 21.

Involving the Total
Organization

The "I told you so" crowd is having a field day proclaiming that the total quality management fad is over. They are saying what they knew all along: *"it was great in the good times but as soon as financial troubles entered it was the first to go."* These nay-sayers have a lot of examples to show to prove their point that when faced with hard times businesses sour on total quality management:[1]

- Florida Power and Light slashed its program after winning the Deming Prize because of worker complaints of excessive paperwork.

- Wallace Company entered Chapter 11 after winning the Baldrige Award.

- At Douglas Aircraft, a subsidiary of McDonnell Douglas Corporation, the program failed because massive layoffs poisoned labor–management relationships.

The authors wish to thank Glen Hoffherr, Founding Principal, Strategic Total Enterprise Management Institute, for his assistance in the preparation of this chapter.

1. The Cost of Quality, *Newsweek*, September 7, 1992, pp. 48–49.

- A Rath and Strong study showed that only 36% of the companies interviewed said that TQM was having an impact.[2]

There is also confusion over what this process is called. Is it total quality

- Leadership?
- Management?
- Ownership?
- Teaming?
- Control?
- Service?
- Involvement?
- Participation?
- Interaction?
- Empowerment?

Every organization wants to personalize the process, so the proliferation of names goes on at a never ending pace. Each new name makes a slight alteration to the definition. They are all trying to define quality, which is what the customer perceives. The customer observes a tangible product every time. This tangible product may be manufactured goods, treatment at a hospital, information from a government agency, education in a school, on the preparation of a legal document. These various industries want to be identified as either manufacturing or service, but in the customer's eye they all deliver a tangible product. Each industry will go to great lengths to show how it is different and that what worked for one in quality will not work for the other. Granted, the definition of customer

---

2. Ibid.

may vary (client, patient, resident, student, and so on), but the basic quality process is still the same.

All these industries, in order to survive, must be customer oriented and provide tangible products that are profitable to the customer and the producing organizations. To be profitable to both requires the providing organization to focus its resources in the most productive manner possible. This focusing process requires an alignment of the business plan, quality plan, strategic plan, research and development plan, and so on. Alignment requires that a leading purpose be established to which all the work of an organization is aligned and designed to achieve.

The problem today is that every organization has so many plans that they compete with one another for the limited resources available. What results is suboptimization. The usual winner is the short-term financial plan. We must keep the shareholders and Wall Street happy even at the expense of the long-term stability of the organization.

Strategic future focus is a concept that blends the critical business systems together in an organization to ensure its long-term survival. The critical business systems are as follows:

- Competitive analysis
- Strategic planning
- Cultural change
- Customer focus
- Daily work management

In many organizations during the initial attempts at total quality management, there is usually misunderstanding about the intent of the program, little top management direct involvement, poor communication, improper implementation, superficial solutions to complex problems, too many plans, the "financial plan always wins in the end" syndrome, and confusion over roles at each level of the organization.

Many questions about roles surface such as the following:

- ✏ What do the CEO and president do?
  - ✗ Become the CTO, Chief Transformation Officer?
  - ✗ Personally lead the effort?
  - ✗ Delegate it?
  - ✗ Form a council to oversee it?
  - ✗ Monitor it?
  - ✗ Observe it?
  - ✗ Keep away from it?

- ✏ Where does it start?
  - ✗ From the top and go down?
  - ✗ From the middle and grow in both directions?
  - ✗ From the bottom and grow upward?
  - ✗ From anywhere in the organization and grow in any direction?

- ✏ What do the middle managers do?
  - ✗ Lead the effort?
  - ✗ Oppose the effort?
  - ✗ Ignore the effort?
  - ✗ Act as facilitators?
  - ✗ Act as coaches

- ✏ How does training happen?
  - ✗ Senior management?
  - ✗ Middle management?

    ✗   Supervision?

    ✗   Human resources?

    ✗   Outside consultants?

   ✏ What do we train in?

    ✗   Process?

    ✗   Problem solving?

    ✗   Teaming?

    ✗   Customer analysis?

   ✏ How do we turn the training into action?

    ✗   Form teams?

    ✗   Individual action?

    ✗   Demand it?

    ✗   Encourage it?

    ✗   Request it?

    ✗   Plead for them?

   ✏ What happens to the recommendations that are made to solve organization problems?

    ✗   Review them?

    ✗   Shelve them

    ✗   Praise them?

    ✗   Ignore them?

    ✗   Act on them?

    ✗   Hope they go away?

Strategic future focus, as shown in Figure 2.1 delineates the responsibilities for critical systems to an organization's long-term survival. The strategic future focus concepts goes beyond the traditional tenants of TQM and looks at ways to grow the business in the future and maintain the current business that we have. Strategic future focus is a process aimed at customer commitment and not just customer satisfaction. Customer commitment is when an organization partners with its current and future customers to develop shared solutions to customer needs. Customer commitment builds loyalty and dependence. The current fad of customer satisfaction is one of pleasing the customer after mistakes are made, correcting deficiencies after the fact, and not building loyalty. Customer commitment requires an organization to take a quantum leap in its customer guarantee policies and to be proactive and not reactive.

Three key responsibilities emerge:

1. *Leadership:* those responsible for the entire system
2. *Management:* those delegated specific systems that deliver tangible products to the organization's customers
3. *Ownership:* those that perform critical processes and tasks that link together to accomplish the delivery of the tangible products

The *leadership* has the responsibility for competitive analysis and strategic planning. The leadership is the group that sets the long-term course of the organization and enables and assists the rest of the organization to accomplish it. The leadership explains, councils, and coaches division managers and small business units on how to accomplish the planned direction.

Leadership develops enthusiasm in those below them to accomplish organizational stretch goals. This enthusiasm is developed through trust. This trust is a two-way street. People in the organization trust the leadership to deliver the empowerment and resources for them to accomplish the organiza-

Leadership		Management		Ownership
Competitive analysis	Strategic planning	Cultural change	Customer commitment	Daily work management
• Corporate mirror	• Purpose hierarchy	• Cultural hierarchy	• Current/future profiles	• Critical competencies
• Product bundles	• Prganization evaluation	• Critical cultural delivery systems	• Mutual awareness	• Passion to do it right
• Horizon scan	• Critical purpose factors	• Critical cultural functions	• View us as a strategic resource	• Education and training
• Leverage points	• Critical cultural philosophies	• People	• Internal	• Critical processes
• Gap analysis	• 80/20 reviews	• Systems	• External	• Critical tasks
• Product/service line strategies		• Structures	• Product mapping	• Reengineering
		• Symbols	• Listening for the voice	• Stream/linkage building
				• Empowerment

Figure 2.1 Strategic Future Focus

tional stretch goals that they have established. The leadership must trust the rest of the organization to deliver the accomplishments that they have agreed to in a timely manner.

Leadership in a future-focused organization ensures that people understand what is expected from them, that their actions support it, and that everyone is held accountable for his or her actions. A recent survey[3] showed that most leaders have a long way to go to accomplish these goals. Approximately 50% of those surveyed said that management's actions support the articulated mission. In addition, 8 out of 10 employees said that they are not held accountable for their own daily performance. The results of the survey are shown in Figure 2.2.

Leadership has a duty to monitor and track progress on the agreed to accomplishments. When deviations from the set

Percentage that answered yes among:	Management	Sales/Frontline Employees
Does your company have a clear written mission statement?	97%	77%
Is that statement supported by management actions?	54%	55%
Do all departments, branches, and divisions have specfic measurable goals?	54%	57%
Does every employee understand what is expected in terms of performance?	46%	38%
Are all employees held accountable for daily performance?	21%	22%

Figure 2.2 Reality Check Survey

3. *INC.*, March 1993, vol. 15, no. 3, p. 34.

course are detected, leadership must coach and counsel those below them rather than blame and punish.

Leadership is the conductor of the orchestra. It must orchestrate a clear mandate as to what is to be accomplished. It must share the purpose creation process with the organization so that everyone is playing from the same song sheet.

Management has the responsibility for specific, well-defined critical systems that are vital to the accomplishment of the long-term organizational stretch goals. Management must ensure that they support, train, work, and plan with those involved in their critical systems. Management must focus on the process in their critical system as their first priority and not blame the people in the system.

Management has the important role of changing the organization's culture. The leadership can define what culture is necessary to achieve the organization's purpose. Management has to translate that definition into action. Management develops the tone in the organization. As the leadership conducts the orchestra to a successful performance, management must provide the tones that are necessary to build the base for a successful performance.

Management is the integrator and coordinator in the orchestra and must be skilled in cross-functional management and group dynamics to accomplish their mission. They, like the leadership must tell, do, and perform in the manner that they want others to act.

Management must also build into the cultural change effort a conscious and consistent focus throughout the organization on the customer and its tangible product. They must build efficient systems that regularly monitor, translate, and disseminate the voice of the customer to the rest of the organization.

Ownership focuses on the critical processes and tasks that are performed on a regular daily basis. Ownership focuses everyone in the organization on daily work management.[4] Daily work management is the process of continuous improvement of our work processes and our internal–external customer–supplier relationships. It develops in the individuals in the organization the passion to do their job correctly and efficiently and to be accountable for daily performance.

Ownership is developing a permanent stake in your process and having the ability to change or influence inefficient or incorrect tasks to make them effective ones. Today most individuals in an organization feel that they have a fragmented stake and that important decisions affecting them are made in secret.

For an organization to make a successful transformation to a strategic future-focused environment, everyone involved, leadership, management, and owners, must practice and perform four critical behavioral functions:[5]

- Chosen thought
- Conscious speech
- Consistent action
- Constant care

Chosen thought is focusing on processes, data, perfection, and information sharing. Chosen thought is different from first thinking that people are the problem, but then focusing on the other parameters of a problem situation. Chosen

---

4. J. Moran, C. Collett, and C. Côté, *Daily Management: A System for Individual and Organizational Optimization*, GOAL/QPC, Methuen, Mass., 1990.

5. C. Collett, J. Colletti, J. DeMott, G. Hoffherr, and J. Moran, *Making Daily Management Work: A Perspective for Leaders and Managers*, Goal/QPC, 1992, Methuen, Mass., pp. 125–126.

thought takes time to develop. It comes through practice and patience.

Conscious speech helps us to set the tone for the cultural change that is necessary for the organization to achieve its purpose. When we speak at any level, we focus on improvements, we encourage questions, we discuss critical processes and tasks, and we focus on breakthroughs.

Consistent action is similar to constancy of purpose. Consistent action ensures that we act the way we want others to act and respond. It is not a "do as I say and not as I do" philosophy. It is a true walk the talk action.

Constant care, in a future-focused organization, is the careful nurturing of all those involved in the change process to ensure them that they are on the right course and providing resources and training and rewards and recognition for appropriate behavior and team accomplishments.

To be able to exhibit the preceding behaviors on a regular basis, leaders, managers, and owners need to develop a series of separate but interrelated skills and attitudes. Training in these skills and attitudes must be rigorous and challenging and not academic and abstract. The training must be genuinely useful and challenge their imagination.

Figure 2.3 shows the most critical of these skills and attitudes. In all three areas of responsibilities shown, it is assumed that the following basic competencies are in place:

- Efficient data-driven decision making

- Long-term commitment

- Dedication to achieving the strategic plan

- Role model at all levels: tell, do, and perform

- Effective information sharing

Leadership	Management	Ownership
• Focus on humanware	• Facilitate action	• Endless enthusiasm
• Change master	• Focus on organization goals	• Motivated
• Develop strategic capability	• Coordinator/integrator	• Effecient time management
• Conflict resolution	• Skilled in group dynamics	• Assertive
• Articulate clear mandates and purpose	• Negotiator	• Negotiator
• Global perspective	• Influencer	• Problem solvers
• Environmental adaption	• Coalition builder	• Customer value orientation
• Convert customers	• Orchestrate versus tell	• Proactive in improving daily work
• Efficient decision maker	• Data-based decisions	• Expertise and specialization
• Franchise others	• Efficient decision maker	• Team player
• Display creativity	• Do, tell, perform	• Dedication
• Lobby skills	• Collaborative skills	
• Focus on quality, finance, and relationships	• Recognize and encouage	
• Effective information manager	• Team player	
	• Commitment to the team concept	

Figure 2.3 Interrelated Skills and Attitudes: Think What To Do Rather Than How To Do It

Example of Repositioning TQM for Breakthrough Results

Like many companies, Galileo Electro-Optics Corporation of Sturbridge, Massachusetts, has been on the TQM crusade. Galileo realized some of the anticipated benefits of their quality efforts; however, these improvements were not occurring at a pace rapid enough to support their defense- to commercial-business conversion. Galileo did not have the luxury of 10 years to implement quality; they needed breakthroughs in quality now.

As part of their reengineering efforts, Galileo redefined TQM and developed framework and implementation approaches to suit their specific needs. This reengineering effort at Galileo is shown in Figure 2.4.

Galileo's TQM framework incorporates three major elements:

1. The *customer*, which provides the focus for Galileo's TQM efforts via the customer's defined (spoken, known) and anticipated (unspoken, unknown) requirements

2. The execution process, or an integrated set of tools, techniques, methodologies, and reengineered business processes aimed at achieving breakthrough

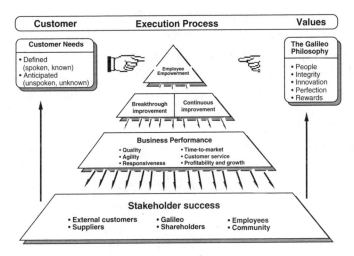

Figure 2.4   Galileo's TQM Framework

improvement and continuous improvement through
employee empowerment and self-managed cross-
functional work teams

3. The *values*, or the beliefs, convictions, and cultural
    climate that facilitates change and determines the
    velocity, magnitude, and rate of success (the Galileo
    philosophy).

The foundation of Galileo's renewed TQM framework is
stakeholder success. Stakeholders include ultimate customers,
the company, its employees, suppliers, and shareholders, and
the community. Success is defined as meeting or exceeding
stakeholder expectations, and implies stretching beyond traditional customer satisfaction measures. Stakeholder success is
the underpinning of Galileo's TQM framework. Quality (or
corporate existence) is meaningless unless all stakeholders are
successful. A satisfied customer with an unprofitable company,
unhappy employees, and adversarial suppliers does not consti-
tute quality.

Employee empowerment drives the TQM process. Employees are the enablers of stakeholder success; it is the employees
who anticipate needs, respond via a set of values and beliefs,
and execute change. Every employee is responsible for the
quality of his or her immediate area and is also encouraged to
identify and pursue opportunities outside of the immediate
area.

Employees are directed by customer need. Internally,
employees are aware of their customer/supplier relationships
and view themselves as both a customer and a supplier. Externally, employees are aware of customer needs and often participate jointly in defining and meeting needs.

Employees are also directed by the Galileo philosophy. This
is a set of corporate beliefs and principles that defines Galileo's

culture and provides a philosophy for managing the business. The Galileo philosophy provides a form, shape, and substance of behavior and includes statements about people, integrity, innovation, perfection, and rewards.

Galileo seeks to improve business performance in every aspect of the business. Stakeholder success is dependent on perfection in quality, agility, flexibility and responsiveness, value-added customer services, and business performance. Customer success is achieved by bringing the Galileo philosophy to life (people, integrity, innovation, perfection, and rewards).

Within the execution process are breakthrough improvement and continuous improvement. This is the collection of process reengineering, prevention-based TQM tools and techniques, and facilitation skills that employees have received through several formal education programs. These skills are the employee's tools of the trade that enable ongoing revolutionary and continuous improvement that ultimately leads to stakeholder success.

This renewed TQM framework provides a common language that focuses on a common direction and an integrated set of values. It also communicates that linkages and successes in every element create a multiplier effect for the corporation. While Galileo's previous quality efforts were impressive, they have achieved industry breakthroughs in fiber-optic quality during the last year that have positioned them as the performance leader.

In a future-focused organization we are simultaneously implementing the strategy, cultural change, operational improvements, and upgrading of skills to optimize our intellectual capital's ability to achieve the organization's stretch goals, which will ensure the organization's long-term survival.

Future-Focused Organization Structure

In the environment of today's rigid organizational structure many good ideas of great promise are abandoned each year because of the difficulty in managing complex organizational relationships. Many of these abandoned ideas are opportunities for increasing customer satisfaction. Organizations that have this problem of abandoning good ideas because of complex relationships usually have an organizational structure akin to a sewer system with two-way flow and many backups.

In a future-focused organization the organizational structure is very lean and is composed of three types of management:

1. Strategic management
2. Lateral management
3. Daily management

This future-focused organization structure allows the organization to act on each good idea to improve relationships and please its customers. This structure reduces complexity and promotes cooperation and collaboration.

A term that can be used to gauge the degree of agility in American industry is *organizational robustness,* the migration toward a flat, fluid boundaryless and seamless organization. Many executives agree with the need to streamline and simplify their organizations, but relatively few companies are making the dramatic structural changes required to make organizational robustness a reality.

Companies are continuing to place priority on employee involvement and empowerment as the number of job classifications and organizational levels shrinks dramatically. Eventually, the steady path of promotion up a hierarchical organization will become a relic, supplanted by a horizontal, fluid fast-track structure that provides valued employees an array of work experiences and more free time. As companies reengineer away their nonvalue-added activities, they will be able to restructure their organizations into boundaryless customer pools that resemble that of a professional services firm. They will also continue to make investments in their people to increase the organization's competency and learning rate. You might be thinking, "This all sounds great, but what does it look like and how does it work?"

In the future-focused organization, there is one single box on the organization chart called the *customer success function.* This function is comprised of critical customer processes (amoeba plots), or fractals of resources assembled on demand to increase customer value. Critical customer processes are comprised of physical and business processes that generate activity in the organization. We often describe these structures as dynamic antibodies (a great pronoun for organizations) that are redeployed to capitalize on market opportunities or to destroy waste. In practice, this redeployment process might resemble a 1960s lava light moving 100 miles per hour! The structure may seem fragmented, unstructured, and confusing. However, this organization is extremely agile, structured, and very disciplined at creating customer success. Figure 3.1 shows an example of an amoeba plot.

Strategic management is one of the permanent structures in the organization that focuses on developing the strategic goals of the organization, deploying them to all the daily management work units, and reviewing progress on meeting these goals. Strategic management develops three types of goals:

1. Efficiency goals, related to resource utilization

2. Effectiveness goals, related to customer commitment

3. Flexibility Goals, related to responsiveness to change

Strategic management deploys the efficiency and effectiveness goals to the Daily management structure since they have control over the means to accomplish changes in these goals. The flexibility goals are deployed to the lateral management

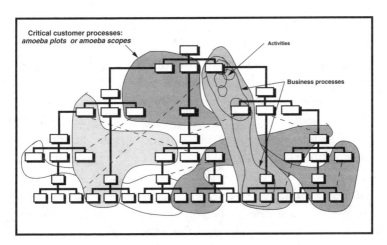

Figure 3.1 Breakthrough! Reengineering the Organization: Customer Success Function

structure since they have the ability and resources to work across the organization to initiate change to accomplish the flexibility goals. Lateral managers help to define the common areas between functional daily managers to improve the flexibility of the organization.

Strategic management focuses on keeping the future-focused organization on the right course. It plans the major shifts in emphasis, tracks the customer's shifting needs and expectations, and plans the major interventions to remain a viable entity in the global marketplace. Strategic managers must work on the common areas that are causing obstacles in the rest of the organization to accomplishing the strategic goals. Strategic managers must help align the routine functional daily work with the strategic effectiveness and efficiency goals. Strategic managers must also develop and put in place the appropriate organizational structure that will help accomplish the strategic goals. If the appropriate organizational structure is not in place, it will create stress in the organization and cause people to work long hours to get work and products completed that still may not satisfy the customer.

The strategic management structure must help the organization to understand that financial goals and organizational goals are not mutually exclusive. One area to help this alignment of financial goals and organizational goals is in the reward system. An organization the authors are familiar with has a gain sharing program that rewards an employee $1200 for achieving the financial goals but only $100 for achieving customer satisfaction goals. Employees in this organization do not see the connection between customer satisfaction and increased sales and loyalty and the achievement of very short-term financial goals. Customers are second-class citizens in this organization.

In a future-focused organization, strategic management is the external and future focus of the organization. This is where the members of the strategic management team spend their time and energy—on the future and the external environment. Strategic managers do not get involved with day-to-day or micromanagement issues. However, they do ensure that the daily management of the organization is aligned to the current and future needs of the organization.

Lateral management is a temporary structure in the organization that focuses on the achievement of corporate-wide flexibility goals and objectives. This form of management is virtual. It comes together as a alliance, as needed, to accomplish important boundary breaking and breakthrough solutions to organization-wide needs. This type of management structure is in the total reengineering business. It works on the system to change the culture to achieve smoother flows through functions that accomplish the "whats" that help achieve ongoing operational goals. Lateral management focuses on the "hows" that make the "whats" happen.

Lateral management assignments will become more attractive to those in the organization since they will be the new route to promotions. Today, middle management jobs are vaporizing at an exponential rate as organizations attempt to become lean, fast acting, and profitable. Lateral management assignments will provide the fast trackers in the organization an opportunity to learn about the complexity of their organization as well as having the feeling of a promotion. The sense of feeling promoted and being valued more is an important element in building a person's self-esteem and loyalty to the organization. Lateral management assignments, even though temporary, will broaden daily managers into strategic managers over time.

Daily management is a permanent but routine structure in the organization that focuses on the routine work that accomplishes the functions that transform inputs into needed and value-added customer products and services. Daily managers focus the ongoing work units on continuous improvement of the routine work processes. Continuous improvement is incremental improvement and is part of the fabric of the way daily work is performed in a future-focused organization.

The focus of this chapter is on lateral management; some organizations practice a form of this under the name of cross-functional management. Chapter 2 focused on the strategic and daily management roles. Daily management, as mentioned in Chapter 2, is composed of functional management and the majority of the organization's associates. Daily management, concerned with the effectiveness and efficiency goals, is internally focused but ready to change as the organization moves forward.

The three types of management structure in a future-focused organization are shown in Figure 3.2.

The characteristics of lateral management are as follows:

Figure 3.2   Management Structure

- A management involvement activity based on inter divisional cooperation

- A horizontal integration process to help an organization achieve efficient organization-wide stretch flexibility goals

- Organizational barrier breaking approach that reduces complex layering

- A way to expand the scope of strategic activities and actions

- A process to deploy some of the top management's functions

- A cultural change agent

- A process to expand the empowerment concept

- A process to define the common ground between functional units to smoothly facilitate the flow of horizontal work

The lateral relationships are complex because the exercise of power and the authority to maintain and protect the vertical boundaries of turf are constantly working against it. Reward structures also complicate smooth lateral relationships since individual performance is more prized than cooperation and team work.

Today we force these lateral or cross-functional relationships by using executive power and authority. These forced lateral relationships are often based on urgency or survival and produce short-term results with disastrous long-term consequences.

A future-focused organization has long learned through experience that the old approach of looking for culprits and punishing them for problems is not effective.

In a future-focused organization, major problems are approached in a lateral manner because the organization's memory tells those in authority that a lateral alliance is an effective way to solve major problems, since innovation happens quicker, change is accomplished faster, implementation is smoother, and ownership is widespread. Figure 3.3 shows this relationship.

In a future-focused organization, decision makers charged with managing change that is complex do not go it alone. They become effective influencers. They seek out those with the useful ideas and knowledge in the organization. They actively seek both their active involvement along with their ideas and views even if they are counter to their own or controversial.

A future-focused organization's decision makers know that people have ownership in relationships and processes for which they have shared in the creation, and they do not leave these to chance. They know that lateral management decision makers in future-focused organizations have five major responsibilities in any lateral management alliance that they lead:

1. Define purpose and goals
2. Create a new atmosphere and new behaviors
3. Develop knowledge and learning
4. Establish accountability and control
5. Document and review progress on a regular basis

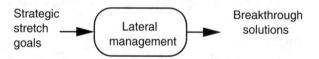

Figure 3.3   Results of Lateral Management

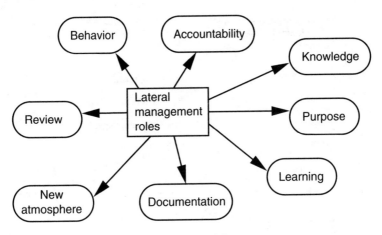

Figure 3.4 Lateral Manager's Responsibilities

Figure 3.4 shows the complexity of a lateral manager's job.

Lateral managers are alliance builders who influence others in the organization to work together as a team to accomplish organizational goals and objectives. Lateral managers have to create the right atmosphere for those on the lateral level to function and accomplish their purpose. Lateral managers have to balance the needs of the lateral team with the needs of the organization. Lateral managers work with team members who come from different sections of the organization with different cultures, and they need to integrate the best of similarities and differences to push the lateral team forward with minimal internal conflicts to accomplish their goals. Figure 3.5 shows the four major areas that they must balance to accomplish the team's purpose.

To develop a smooth-flowing lateral team, lateral managers need to focus their future-focused organization on the following four areas as the main elements of their job:

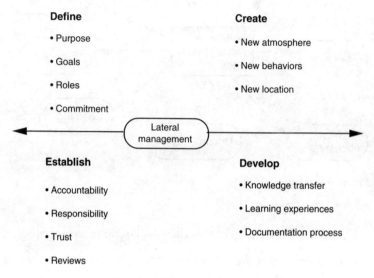

Define

• Purpose

• Goals

• Roles

• Commitment

Create

• New atmosphere

• New behaviors

• New location

Lateral management

Establish

• Accountability

• Responsibility

• Trust

• Reviews

Develop

• Knowledge transfer

• Learning experiences

• Documentation process

Figure 3.5   Four Major Areas of Lateral Management

1. *Define*

A. Purpose:

✗   The reason for the existence of lateral team must be defined.

✗   The benefit ratio for the project to be undertaken must be stated.

B. Goals:

✗   What is expected of this lateral management team must be clearly stated.

✗   The boundaries of the project must be defined.

✗ The expectations of management must be detailed.

C. Roles:

✗ Management must define the structure of lateral teams.
✗ Management must define the general roles of each position on a lateral management team.
✗ Management must define its role.

D. Commitment: management questions:

✗ How will management show commitment?
✗ How will we reward lateral teams?
✗ How will we support lateral teams?
✗ How much empowerment will we sanction?

2. *Create*

A. New atmosphere:

✗ Trust
✗ Reduce confusion
✗ Create enthusiasm
✗ Truthful
✗ Cooperative
✗ Competence
✗ Humility
✗ Stress free
✗ Ownership
✗ Clear focus: purpose
✗ Nonnegotiating: no trading favors
✗ Noncompetitive

- ✗ Open and collaborative
- ✗ Win–win situations
- ✗ Sense of urgency, importance of the project or program, high organization priority
- ✗ Wide spread involvement of the organization, honestly seek inputs from a wide section of the Organization

B. New behaviors:

- ✗ Sense of purpose
- ✗ Surface hidden conflicts
- ✗ Focus on process (root cause) not people
- ✗ Supportive of peers
- ✗ Jointly define roles, processes, relationships, and expected results
- ✗ Cooperation rather than competition
- ✗ Keep promises
- ✗ Follow through on commitments
- ✗ Admit errors
- ✗ Use influence rather than power and authority
- ✗ Free to express ideas

C. New location:

- ✗ Establish a co-location for the lateral management team
- ✗ Eliminate functional barriers by moving team members to a common location
- ✗ Co-location allows for a free flowing interaction that builds trust

- ✗ Co-location helps create interdependencies; we need each other to survive
- ✗ Co-location increases productivity; no need for meetings to pull the team together, we are together all the time
- ✗ Co-location contributes to the trust building process
- ✗ Co-location contributes to smooth information low

3. *Develop*

   A. Knowledge to transfer:

   - ✗ Integrate alliance members with different perspectives
   - ✗ Integrate alliance members with different demonstrated competencies
   - ✗ Common consensus decision-making process to integrate alliance members with different decision-making skills
   - ✗ Alliance members educate each other
   - ✗ Why we use lateral teams: innovation happens faster, training on innovation[1]
   - ✗ How to make collaboration work
   - ✗ Creative ways to innovation: new tools

   B. Learning experiences:

   - ✗ Always interested in learning
   - ✗ Always open to learning

---

1. G. Hoffherr, J. Moran, and G. Nadler, *Breakthrough Thinking in Total Quality Management*, Prentice Hall PTR, Englewood Cliffs, N.J., 1994.

    ✗ Learn from our own and other team's mistakes

    ✗ Learn from each other

    ✗ Learn from others outside our group

    ✗ Learn a common problem-solving methodology

    ✗ Learn consensus decision making

    ✗ Learn communication skills

C. Documentation process:

    ✗ Understand processes we are working on

    ✗ Understand our cross-functional management process

    ✗ Understand our successes and failures

    ✗ Understand our progress to our goal

    ✗ Understand the customer needs and wants

    ✗ Understand our needs and wants

4. *Establish*

A. Accountability:

    ✗ Set group goals, not individual

    ✗ Communicate needs clearly

    ✗ Set group structure

    ✗ Shared responsibility for achievement

    ✗ Develop time lines

    ✗ Sub goals achievement

B. Responsibility:

    ✗ Define who is the lateral team leader

    ✗ Define the lateral team leader's roles and responsibilities

✗ Define the lateral team member's roles and responsibilities

C. Trust:

✗ Trust is the key ingredient to a smooth-functioning lateral team

✗ Trust cannot be decreed; it must develop

✗ Management must supply the necessary environment and support for the development of trust

✗ Trust is a fragile commodity, easily broken and difficult to rebuild

✗ Trust development is a key responsibility of the lateral team leader

D. Reviews:

✗ Objective self-evaluation

✗ How we are doing as a lateral team?

✗ How we are doing on our task?

✗ How do others perceive us as a team?

✗ How are we exercising our empowerment?

✗ What has worked well? Why?

✗ What have been our failures? Why?

✗ How can we transfer our reflections to other lateral teams?

Lateral management is the change agent process for a future-focused organization. Lateral managers are rotated through this management structure to receive a broadening view of the organization and to gain the skills of influencing without authority.

Competitiveness	Growth
• Customer service	• Regulatory compliance
• Organization excellence	• International competitiveness
• Technological innovation	• Marketing capability
• New product development	• Organizational barriers
• Time to manufacture	• Overhead
• Time to market	• Health care cost
• Strategic partnerships	

Figure 3.6   Lateral Management Typical Issues

Lateral managers focus on flexibility issues of competitiveness and issues that retard growth. Typical issues that are focused on in each category are shown in Figure 3.6.

A recent survey[2] reported that the top issue that could improve competitiveness is customer service, while the main barrier to growth is regulatory requirements. Both of these issues can be handled efficiently in a lateral management structure since they are company wide in scope.

The first of these lateral management structures has shown up in the automotive industry in the form of platform teams. Chrysler used the platform team approach to develop the Viper sports car from scratch in just 3 years.

A recent analysis of Deming Prize winners in Japan[3] showed that the main results after the introduction of cross-functional or lateral management were as follows:

2. From Debate To Dialogue, Special Advertising Supplement, *Research and Development Magazine*, July 1993.
3. Kozo Koura, An Analysis of the Deming Prize Winners: The Importance of Cross-functional Management In Improving Corporate Health and Character, Abstracts of the EOQ '93 World Quality Congress, Helsinki, Finland, June 1993.

- Strengthened cooperation between divisions
- Reduction of process defects and defect losses
- Expansion and improved sales of new products
- Increases in net sales, numbers of products, and number of customers
- Reduction of claims and customer inconveniences

The lateral management structure is a temporary alliance that is built and nurtured to achieve its stated purpose and then disbanded. Lateral mangers then go back into a position in either of the two permanent paths of the organization, strategic management or daily management. The permanency of the strategic management and daily management structures is usually measured in terms of years. Strategic management and daily management are semipermanent in that they can be changed or modified as an organization's needs, purpose, and objectives change.

To accomplish this integrated, smooth-flowing alliance building, a lateral manager may employ a lateral flow chart to show the interrelationships of the various functions being represented on the lateral team. Figure 3.7 shows a lateral flow chart in macro detail. The flows and interrelationships from each function would have to be drawn in.

A lateral flow chart is an illustration of the sequence of functions that make up a lateral alliance. These functions are arranged in a functional grid showing the flow of proposed activities to accomplish a flexibility goal through the functions represented on the alliance.

The flow chart is used as follows:

- To allow members of each function represented to see their precise role in the alliance
- To show hand-offs from one functional unit to another

Lateral goal _____

Functions

F 1	F 2	F 3	F 4	F 5

Figure 3.7   Lateral Flow Chart

- To provide a starting point for various other detailed descriptions and analyses, such as responsibility charts, competency charts, or cost and cycle-time charts

Process Steps

Step 1. Mark a large sheet of paper into columns; each column represents one of the functions involved in the process.

Step 2. Flow chart the sequence of proposed activities to be accomplished. Use typical flow-chart symbols to represent the various proposed activities. Use arrows to show the interrelationship between functions.

Step 3. Transfer the proposed activities and arrows to the appropriate functional columns

Step 4. Identify any activities that are currently not performing up to standard. (Use systematically collected data when possible to determine this.)

✗ What outputs/requirements are not performing well?

✗ What activities are likely to be involved in these outputs?

✗ Aside from their relation to output, what activities are troublesome?

Step 5. Analyze the flow of activity to see how the activities can be made more efficient and effective.

✗ What steps can be combined or eliminated?

✗ What steps tend to be bottlenecks?

✗ Where can concurrent engineering be applied (doing multiple activities at once)?

✗ Where are the long feedback loops? Can anything be done to eliminate or shorten them?

Step 6. If you have not done so already, explore performance levels through available measurements.

✗ How is the process currently measured? What do the measures tell you about the process's performance?

✗ How much time does the process take?

✗ How consistently does the process produce the output your customers want?

The organizational structure in a future-focused organization must not become an extended bureaucracy, but be a flexible, fluid, and virtual one that responds quickly to a changing market environment and customers. A key to accomplishing this flexible but fluid organization is lateral management.

Lateral Management Summary

1. Lateral management teams are formed for the purpose of managing an issue critical to the success of the organization across the various functions and business units of the company. Secondarily, lateral management helps create broader perspectives for future general managers.

2. Lateral management teams are led by a member of senior management and comprised of management committee members. Each lateral management team reports to the management committee. Each lateral team has a facilitator and requires staff support from related functions. For example, to prepare for its monthly meeting, a lateral team on customer satisfaction may require some information from customer relations or marketing, who would prepare the information and present it to the committee at their meeting.

3. Lateral management teams can have permanent, full-time members or it could be composed of members who are part-time and meet on the average 3 to 4 hours weekly, although this may vary by phase of work or nature of the issue. It is best if the members are full-time and permanent, since they will devote their full time and energy to important company-wide goals. If the goal is really important to the future of the organization, the more the need for permanent, full-time members.

4. Lateral management teams can form process improvement teams from time to time on an as-needed basis. These are not permanent teams, and in

general they will be led by a member of the lateral management team (when issues are very technical or beyond the expertise of the team, a leader not on the lateral management team may be picked). Members of the process improvement team will come from the functions most affected by the targeted process.

5. Lateral management teams realize that primary responsibility for implementation of the cross-functional goals lies with the daily management structure. Their job is therefore to recommend and monitor progress through the management committee and departmental objectives.

6. Lateral management teams recommend that certain activities be cascaded down through the organization and monitor progress and report to the management committee from an overall company point of view. Lateral management teams recommend overall policy changes and ways to remove obstacles to the process working from an overall company point of view.

7. Lateral management teams may also involve themselves from time to time in the management review process so that company-wide issues are adequately conveyed and discussed as associate members of the review team, or in some cases an independent cross-functional management review could be an option.

8. The key focus of a lateral team leader is the building of trust in the alliance she or he is leading. Trust building is a task that requires an enormous amount of time and energy from a lateral team leader. A lateral team leader must focus on six key areas in building trust in a collaborative atmosphere, as shown in Figure 3.8.

Figure 3.8   Building Trust in a Collaborative Environment

Trust is not the same as trading favors, utilizing past relationships, or calling in a debt that is due. Trust is more than just being honest. Trust is a process of being able to depend on other team members for help, support, knowledge, companionship, and friendship. It is a bond that develops around mutual supportiveness. This trust bond is very fragile, unstable, easily broken, and difficult to repair. The lateral team leader must spend time and energy building the team's commitment to the six key areas shown in Figure 3.8 in order to build a strong bond of trust.

These six key areas can be defined as follows:

1. *Attitude:* Lateral team members exhibit an internal and external noncompetitive attitude toward each other in all interactions. This noncompetitive attitude helps to improve the free flow of information

vital to learning about the project assigned and making lasting change.

2. *Collaboration:* Lateral team members freely and willingly share their skills and expertise with each other and those outside the team.

3. *Joint accountability:* Lateral team members understand that this is a joint venture and not a solo flight. There is no individual glory or blame in this process. We need each other to survive and complete our assignment.

4. *Acknowledgment:* Lateral team members must acknowledge errors or mistakes freely, as well as acknowledge uncertainties. There can be no bluffing in a lateral team environment.

5. *Commitment:* Lateral team members must be personally committed to this process and believe in teamwork. There is no place for hidden agendas. Egos must be put away.

6. *Cooperation:* Lateral team members must follow through on their promises, assignments, or duties. Team members were selected because they are the best and must demonstrate a cooperative spirit.

Lateral team leaders have to nurture this trust-building bond process in a short period of time since lateral projects are virtual and finite. To expedite this process, the lateral team leader, working with the team members, should develop at the outset of the project a set of shared values focused on the six key areas defined. It is essential for the lateral team leader to seek an agreement from the team on how they will work consciously to honor the agreements on the shared values developed. These agreements become the "hows" of accomplishing the "whats" that have been assigned.

The lateral team leader must audit how the team is doing on the agreements and understand how well the lateral team's internal process of working together is doing in a real-time sense. Figure 3.9 shows the six key areas of trust building with a rating scale.

The team leader at regular intervals should pull the team together and have an open and honest discussion on how they are doing on meeting their agreements and commitments. The lateral team leader can rate each one of the six categories shown in Figure 3.9 individually and then have an open discussion to come to a consensus decision on where they are.

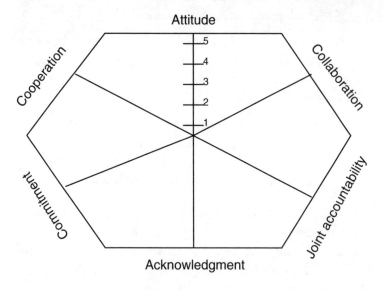

1. low, little progress
3. some improvement
5. world class lateral team

Figure 3.9   Rating the Key Areas of Trust

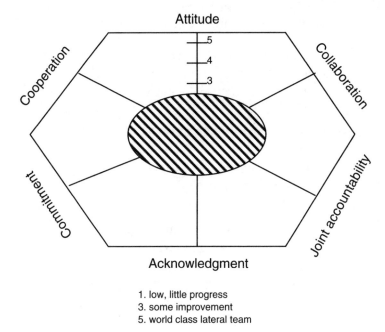

Figure 3.10 A Rating Plot

Each score should have a "why," the reason for the score, associated with it.

Figure 3.10 shows a hypothetical rating for a lateral team. This score would probably be for a lateral team that is very new and just starting the process. The lateral team leader should discuss each score with the team members and the reason for the score in detail. For each low score an action plan should be drafted to deal with the issues raised and improve the score in the near term. Individual as well as group responsibilities may be assigned to make the changes required. This process of checking on agreements gives the lateral team leader the pulse of the team and allows for timely intervention. As the team matures, this process can be more of an audit to ensure that the team is functioning appropriately.

1. Being on a lateral management team is a risk for team members since there are a lot of potential failure points. Senior management must be constantly in touch with lateral management teams that they have initiated to ensure that they are functioning smoothly. Senior management must help lateral teams by removing obstacles and providing needed resources. Lateral management teams will not survive unless they are nurtured.

2. Successful lateral management requires behavioral changes as well as organizational changes. Organizational changes can be made very quickly, but behavioral changes take time and nurturing. Lateral management helps to break down the traditional functional stovepipe barriers that impede smooth-flowing and collaborative work in the organization. Lateral management is designed to reduce the vertical chimney dictator syndrome shown in Figure 3.11.

However, a company that transforms to a lateral management structure without changing any of the behaviors of those involved may wind up with a structure as shown in Figure 3.12.

If the company does not change the mentality and associated behaviors of those involved, it will end up with horizontal dictators instead of vertical chimney dictators. Organizations have experimented with the concept shown in Figure 3.12 on the daily work level by organizing around processes without any attention to the behavior changes that are needed by those involved. These organizations have been amazed at how fast vertical chimney dictators made the change to horizontal pro-

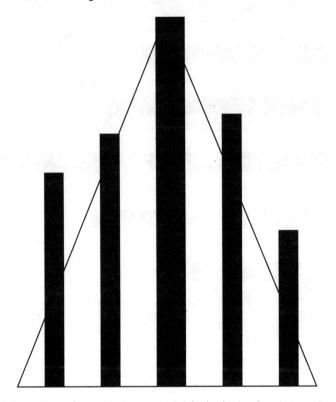

Figure 3.11   Typical Stovepipe Organization

cess czars. These organizations still have the same problems as before, they are now just organized differently.

Successful lateral management, at any level in the organization, requires attention to the six key behavioral changes detailed earlier:

- Attitude
- Collaboration
- Joint accountability
- Acknowledgment

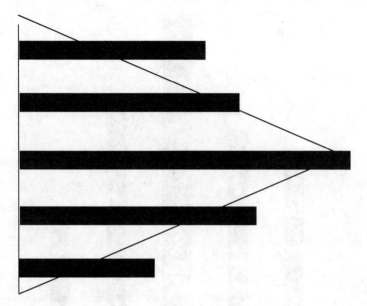

Figure 3.12   Horizontal Stovepipe Organization

- Commitment
- Cooperation

Attention to these behavioral change areas plus the reward and recognition structure that supports lateral management helps to ensure successful change. The process of changing from authority and control to consensus and collaboration as a regular way of running a business requires more than just tipping the organization on its side and calling it lateral management.

The Omni Pattern

Organization culture is difficult to define and understand. Culture is not tangible, yet it influences our decision making and behavioral style. Ask any two individuals in an organization to define their culture and you will have two different definitions. Ask a hundred individuals in the organization and you will have a hundred different definitions. Culture is not only not tangible, but it is very difficult to define.

Culture surrounds an organization like an invisible gas. This gas causes people in the organization to behave in a specific manner. This invisible cultural gas is very impervious to change and thrives in a state of status quo. Culture is so pervasive that sometimes we do not even recognize its existence or impact on our organization.

Culture works behind the scenes in the organization; it is the unwritten but cherished code of conduct of doing business everyday in the organization. The impact of the culture that we feel in an organization is composed of the following factors:

- *People* who work in the organization.

- *Processes* that support the people who work in the organization; how we get work accomplished

- *Regulations,* written and unwritten rules and procedures

- *Visible symbols,* office layouts, work uniforms, corporate logos, and so on

Culture is the sum of these major factors that cause people in the organization to exhibit a certain pattern of overt behaviors, mental habits, and acceptable emotional responses on a regular basis. After a while these overt behaviors, when practiced long enough, become habitual behaviors and require a great deal of management resolve to change. Changing a learned behavior such as eating a certain way, speaking a certain way, or walking a certain way is very difficult. Changing the culture is even more difficult since we have taught people in the organization to behave a certain way and we have rewarded them when they behave that way. The reward structure compounds the difficulty of making change. The reward system makes culture resistant to change.

People in an organization learn how to behave in the appropriate manner by watching successful role models and through training, and the reward system. Changing the culture must be accomplished by a change in all three of these factors. Changing a culture is a long process since we must change deep-rooted convictions. These convictions are composed of core organizational principles, belief systems, and ghosts of past influential managements.

Organizational Patterns Of
Growth and Decline

During the past 10 years we have seen a number of industry giants experience difficult times: layoffs, reorganizations, take-overs, chapter 11, and so on. These giants were not able to change in time to ward off the disasters they were steaming into. In reviewing their past 10-year slide, a four-phase pattern was noticed covering the period from start-up to their current troubled times. These four phases are as follows:

1. Omnipotential
2. Omnicompetent
3. Omnicomplacent
4. Omnislide

The characteristics of the first phase are as follows:

Omnipotential Phase

- Embryo
- Unbridled optimism
- Loose
- What structure?
- Direct access to boss
- Suffer and celebrate together
- I can see and touch the whole company
- Fluid
- I know our customer
- Compete with usefulness and uniqueness

- *We will be better and bigger than IBM!*

The characteristics of the second phase are as follows:

Omnicompetent Phase

- We are king—take it or go some place else
- Highly automated
- New people, new views, new values
- From discrete units to stovepipes
- More chiefs and less indians
- Rigidity starts to set in
- Customers are faceless purchase orders
- Creativity is constrained and not rewarded
- Systems are now the problems
- Promotion of the incompetent
- Add wasteful activities, internal checks
- Educate everyone on anything

- *We will be as big as a division of IBM!*

The characteristics of the third phase are as follows:

Omnicomplacent Phase

- We have gotten big; jigsaw, many pieces not fitting together well
- Introduce maintenance system programs, maintain the status quo
- Boss is invisible
- Who is the boss?
- Inflexible, very rigid, lots of stovepipes
- What are we?
- Who is the customer?
- Status quo is ok
- I am not heard
- Boss gets big reward; we are lucky to get cost of living

- Compete on cost reductions, zero-sum game
- Educate only on what we think will hold the maturity
- Series of new leaders or champions

- *We are as big as a division of IBM. Now what do we do?*

The characteristics of the fourth and final phase are as follows:

Omnislide Phase

- Dispare
- Panic
- Suspicion
- Slash and burn
- Cut the most essential resources
- Limited choices, made by external forces
- Painful time
- Organization suffers
- Indians suffer
- Families suffer
- Best leave
- Leaders are still rewarded
- Realize we do not know who our customer is
- Grab a quality philosophy
- Try to destroy the culture
- Resistance
- Distrust
- Back to basics, whatever that was
- Education is cut to the bone, it becomes a perk
- Change is destructive, reactive, and incomplete

- *IBM just bought us. Now what do we do?*

This four-phase cycle is being played out in the pages of the business sections of our newspapers everyday. In the past, organizations could focus on changing a culture over a long-term. This long-term view was acceptable since business conditions were predictable and our customer was obvious. Our customer bought what we made. "Any color as long as it is black."

Today we are beginning to live in the zero lead time era. Organizations are going to have to be able to change rapidly in order to survive. This ability for quick change applies to all our institutions—business, government, education, labor unions, and so on.

This rapid change will directly affect the organization's culture since it will also have to change rapidly. We are in for an era of rapid change both in structure and culture. Those that do not change will watch from the sidelines as their influence and market share disappear.

The winners in the next 20 years will be those organizations who can change traditional principles and replace them with new ones that radically change how products and services are designed and delivered, how customers are satisfied and retained, how work is accomplished, and how people are managed.

In the four phase patterns just described, there are commonalties that can be categorized as the six dimensions of any organization. These six organizational dimensioning characteristics are shown in Figure 4.1.

Future-Focused Organization

The organizations that will be the dominant forces in the next 20 years are those that are future focused. Future-focused organizations will have the following characteristics:

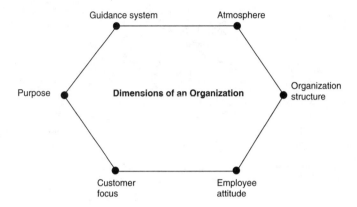

Figure 4.1 Dimensioning the Organization

- They will know how their work is accomplished through their systems by understanding and focusing on the following:

    ✗ Critical purpose factors

    ✗ Critical systems

    ✗ Critical processes

    ✗ Critical tasks

- They will know how their culture influences the ways that work is accomplished by also understanding and focusing on the following:

    ✗ Critical cultural philosophies

    ✗ Critical cultural delivery systems

    ✗ Critical cultural functions

- They will Reengineer or eliminate what is not identified as critical tasks or critical cultural activities.

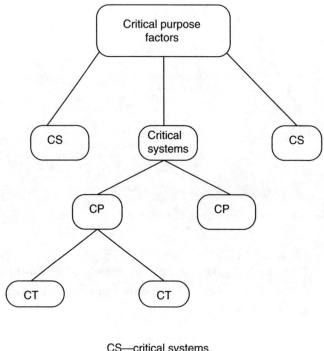

CS—critical systems
CP—critical processes
CT—critical tasks

Figure 4.2   Critical Purpose Factors

The future-focused organization will be a lean organization focused on its purpose[1] and one that has derived its organizational structure from its critical systems and its critical cultural philosophies. Figure 4.2 shows how critical systems[2] flow from the critical purpose factors in a vertical direction.

1. G. Hoffherr, J. Moran, and G. Nadler, *Breakthrough Thinking in Total Quality Management,* Prentice Hall PTR, Englewood Cliffs, N.J., 1994.
2. C. Collett, J. DeMott, and J. Moran, *Critical Processes Application Report,* GOAL/QPC, Methuen, Mass., 1992.

Definitions

The critical purpose factors are as follows:

- ☞ Critical business necessary to achieve the agreed upon purpose of the organization
- ☞ What needs to be different in the future than today
- ☞ How to run the organization to achieve its purpose
- ☞ Related to accomplishing the purpose's objective
- ☞ Cover all aspects of the business
- ☞ Usually a maximum of five
- ☞ Items that can be deployed to and interpreted by the operating and support functions and not just the domain of senior management
- ☞ Achievement possibilities

Definition of Critical Processes and Systems[3]

Critical processes (CPs) are those important sets of procedures or patterns of tasks that determine success (that is, customer satisfaction) for an organization or for an individual's job. At the executive level, some CPs may be quite broad and comprehensive. Therefore, it may be helpful to think in terms of *critical systems,* which are a collection of CPs that must occur simultaneously across the organization. One such critical system is the human resource system, which may consist of a number of CPs, such as hiring, training, development, recognition, and compensation. Critical processes and systems are essential to the *position,* not the *person.* Often, jobs or even whole departments are shaped by the abilities, talents, and preferences of the

---

3. C. Collett, J. DeMott, and J. Moran, *Critical Processes Application Report,* GOAL/QPC, Methuen, Mass., 1992, pp. 1–3.

people hired into the positions. It is necessary to consider each process within each position and to think through the contribution that the process makes to the entire operation.

Attributes of Critical Processes And Systems

1. They are few in number.
2. They are linked, both horizontally and vertically.
3. They can be mapped or diagrammed.
4. They can be measured.
5. They can be standardized and controlled.
6. They can be improved.

Figure 4.3 shows how the cultural system is derived from the critical purpose factors. The cultural system affects the organization in a vertical manner.

Reengineering and Focusing the Culture

The purpose of an organization is derived from the purpose hierarchy, as shown in Figure 4.4. In this chapter we will not go into detail concerning the purpose, critical purpose factors, critical systems, critical processes, and critical tasks since they are detailed in the references given in footnotes 1 and 2. We will concentrate on the cultural hierarchy as shown in Figure 4.5.

Defining the Culture to Support the Organization's Purpose

Once an organization fully understands its purpose, the appropriate culture can be derived from that purpose. As shown in Figure 4.5 the cultural hierarchy is an open cylinder at the top and bottom. We constantly add new cultural systems and drop those systems that are blocking our transition to the next level of our purpose hierarchy. This process helps us to formulate the culture necessary to support the attainment of our purpose.

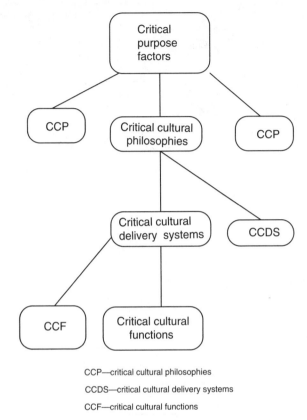

CCP—critical cultural philosophies

CCDS—critical cultural delivery systems

CCF—critical cultural functions

Figure 4.3   Ingraining the Appropriate Organizational Culture

Critical systems affect the organization in a vertical manner, while critical cultural philosophies affect the organization in a horizontal manner. Just as the critical systems are deployed vertically to their critical tasks, so are critical cultural philosophies deployed horizontally to their critical cultural functions.

TQM efforts today have stalled in many organizations because they have tried to deploy the concepts of quality customer satisfaction, empowerment, teaming, and so on, as critical systems, rather than as horizontal critical cultural systems.

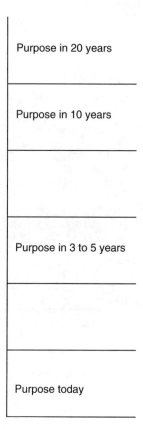

Figure 4.4   Purpose Hierarchy

Chapter 6 will explore the interaction of critical systems and critical cultural philosophies and how this interaction can produce a synergistic effect to move a future-focused organization closer toward its chosen purpose.

Figure 4.6 shows the interaction of critical systems and critical cultural philosophies. If there is not a positive synergistic effect, then a conflict arises that needs to be overcome. Negative effects must be addressed and resolved before any action is initiated.

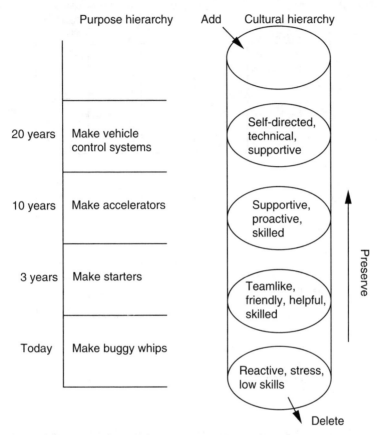

Figure 4.5 Future-Focused Organization Hierarchies

If the critical system is controlled vertically by a hierarchical structure that require us to obey and follow orders ("always check first") and the organization is espousing empowerment as a critical cultural philosophy horizontally, then conflict occurs. This conflict will cause pain and stress in the organization if action is initiated to empower people, but the systems are not in place to allow it to happen.

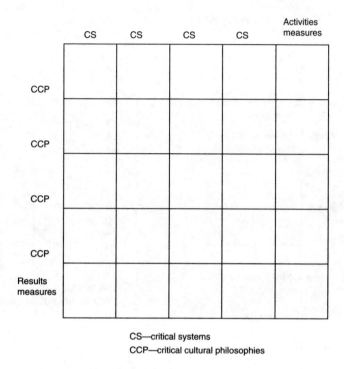

CS—critical systems
CCP—critical cultural philosophies

Figure 4.6 Interaction of Critical Systems and Critical Cultural Philosophies

These conflicts result in stress for those in the system, and they may question the leadership's ability to articulate what it is they want. "They ask me and train me to be empowered but in reality I have to check first before I do anything." The walk and talk don't match. If this conflict is not resolved, it can result in organizational gridlock. Organizational gridlock occurs when the critical systems in the organization are not in sync with the critical cultural philosophies.

Status Quo

Culture likes a steady-state atmosphere to entrench itself and can tolerate a few extreme subcultures, as shown in Figure 4.7.

The real old guard group on the left are the entrenched branches of the organization. They have weathered many a change program and are the first to resist anything new that might challenge the status quo. On the right of Figure 4.7 are the rebels or skunkworks. They are the experimenters that want to try new things. They are usually the first to embrace the latest buzz word or technique. They will run training programs on the technique and can usually gather enough interest to sustain the effort for proposed thinking about change until the next new approach is developed. They are the ones reading this chapter who will start drawing cultural hierarchies to explain their organization's current dilemmas.

Between the two sides of Figure 4.7 is the vast majority (90%) of the organization who like the status quo environment. They know how to function in it and get rewarded by it. This group forms the change resistance pocket of the organization.

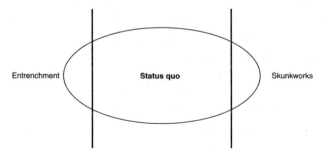

Figure 4.7   A Cultural System

Organizations in the future are going to be forced to change rapidly and must adopt new methods of changing culture other than the catastrophic event and chaotic upheaval approach used today.

Organizations today tend to try to change their culture only when a catastrophic event (market share decline, large losses, takeovers, product failure, and the like) precipitates the need for change. This is usually followed by chaotic upheaval in the organization. We either attack the entrenched group or the skunkworks. The attack pushes hard against one side of the cultural oval—change happens. This push against one side takes a tremendous amount of leadership effort—sometimes a new leader—and cannot be kept up forever. So, like a balloon, once we regain our market share or increase our profits, we tend to relax, and the balloon goes back to its original shape and the status quo returns.

Culture has to be viewed not as an oval that has no opening but as a cylinder, as shown in Figure 4.8. Culture has persuasiveness and depth, both of which we must understand before we make a change. The cylinder is open at the top and bottom to add and delete to it as needed.

Organizations must be constantly on the alert for potential cultural change agents. Potential cultural change agents are external and internal drivers that could cause a chaotic upheaval within the organization.

Some potential cultural change agents are the following:

- Government regulations
- Global political events
- Global competitors
- Union contract negotiations
- Investors

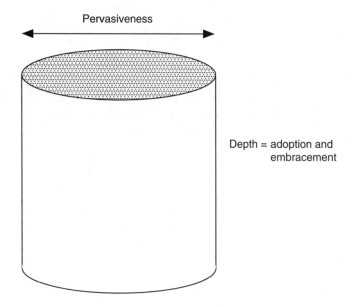

Figure 4.8 Cultural Cylinder

- Mergers and acquisitions
- Work-force needs
- Technological developments

Organizations need to track these, estimate their effect, and develop contingency plans to overcome them or shape them as positive forces to help achieve the future-focused organization's purpose.

Future-focused organizations must develop measurable indicators to detect trends that may have an effect on the desired behaviors it wants its employees to exhibit. New workers that will join the organization in the next 5 to 20 years are having their behaviors shaped now by society. A recent report on the Commerce Department's index of leading social indicators[4] point to a sharp decline in America's cultural values.

Corporate culture has many dimensions. A reengineering tool called the *cultural climate checklist*[5] (see Figure 4.9) is helpful in getting organizations to view themselves along various dimensions of culture and to identify alignment gaps between present and desired performance. Cultural climate mapping is a based on a combination of employee surveys and direct observation of how the organization behaves and adjusts vis-à-vis predetermined cultural dimensions. The purpose of the cultural climate checklist is to recognize the softer, organizational impediments to achieving success through the reengineering of physical or business processes. The cultural climate checklist is used to assess an organization's current readiness to be an agile future-focused organization. The culture of the organization causes people to behave in a certain manner; it is the code of conduct. To change this code of conduct we must understand it in terms of three major change levers. These three levers, *physical, organizational,* and *psychological,* need to be assessed to understand the current strengths and weaknesses of the existing organization's ability to make a quick change to an agile future-focused organization.

The cultural climate checklist is filled out by scoring the organization's current state on each checklist item. The scoring used is as follows:

1 = needs major improvement

3 = needs minor improvement

5 = needs to be preserved in the future culture

---

4. *Time,* March 29, 1993, p. 18.
5. *BreakThrough Reengineering Toolbox,* Center for Excellence in Operations, Nashua, N.H., 1994.

The evaluation criteria shown under each of three categories are the most common ones used, but they need to be modified by the organization to reflect any uniquenesses. The organization should document the reason(s) that the score was based on.

Once the cultural climate checklist is scored and the lowest-scoring items prioritized, an action plan(s) should be developed to initiate the desired change in these items.

It is important that a future-focused organization monitor not only their own internal cultural measures and their industry's changing values and composition, but also society in general. Future-focused organizations must be leaders of social change that will influence how new and current workers will behave and make judgments in the future. The factors that influence workers outside of work also help to shape the judgmental process that they apply at work.

The right behavior in a future-focused organization is not the one that the boss wants, but the one that supports the achievement of the purpose. The right behavior is derived from the interaction of purpose, corporate values, reward structure, continuous improvement, training and education, investment in the organization, and the cultural values of society in general. Figure 4.10 shows these interactions.

If the desired behavior is exhibited and it is the appropriate one that has been derived from the cultural hierarchy to support the purpose, then the desired business results should be achieved.

The future-focused organization *cultural analysis matrix* is a tool to be used in conjunction with the cultural hierarchy shown in Figure 4.6. Cultural analysis matrix is shown in Figure 4.11.

Lever:	Physical	Score	Organizational	Score	Psychological	Score
	Cleanliness		Discipline		Pleasing the customer	
	Orderliness		Accountability		Respect for the individual	
	Care of Equipment		Freedom		Innovation	
	Punctuality		Standardization		Teamwork	
	Safety		Systemization		Growth of the individual	
	Self-control		Authority		Loyalty	
	Efficient use of cash		Coordination of Departments		Space management	
	Resource utilization		Integration of levels		Service to society	
	Quality of product		Communication		Integrity	
	Quality of service		Cooperation		Creativity	
	Time management		Empowerment		Flexibility	
	Self-management		Boundaries			
	Agility					

Figure 4.9   Cultural Climate Checklist

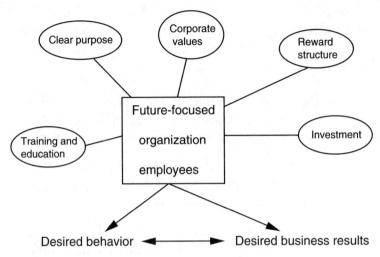

Figure 4.10   Cultural Interactions

Cultural checklist / Cultural position	Preserve	Achieve	Avoid
Current culture	• Cooperative attitude • Friendliness • Helpfulness	• Team spirit • Proactive problem solving • Attention to details	• Stress • Territorial Boundaries • reactive problem solving
Next higher level on the cultural hierarchy	• What we have achieved in our current culture	• Self-directed teaming • Self-learning • Team learning	• Those things that will detract from achieving our future purpose

Figure 4.11   Cultural Analysis Matrix

The purpose of this matrix is to expand the cultural hierarchy by identifying the culture currently in place in the organization in the top half of the matrix. The current culture is broken down into three parts:

1. *Preserve:* culture values and behaviors that are the foundation and will serve as well in the future in pursuing the organization's purpose.

2. *Achieve:* cultural values and behaviors that need to be added to the organization to help it empower our current culture and focus on its purpose.

3. *Avoid:* cultural values and behaviors that no longer serve the organization in a positive manner. If the organization does not avoid or eliminate these cultural values and behaviors, they could seriously undermine the effort to achieve the organization's purpose.

The bottom half of the matrix identifies the next level of the cultural hierarchy that the organization is trying to achieve. The organization needs to identify items that should be transferred from the current culture's preserve and achieve categories to the next cultural level's preserve category. Some of these transferred items may be identified as ones that should be intensified.

The next step is to perform a gap analysis between what has been transferred and what is needed and to itemize those items in the achieve category. If possible, the organization should identify specific cultural values and behaviors that they want to avoid at this next level in their cultural hierarchy. We continue this analysis on to the next level in the cultural hierarchy as required.

Another approach that a future-focused organization can use to monitor potential cultural change agents is the *cultural change agent potential plot* shown in Figure 4.12.

This tool is used by future-focused organizations to monitor change. The cultural change agent plot is a graphic tool to keep an organization focused on potential culture change

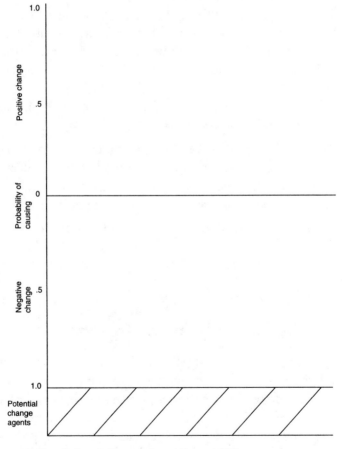

Figure 4.12   Cultural Change Agent Potential Plot

agents that could either positively or negatively affect its current organizational culture. This graphic tool focuses the leaders of a future-focused organization on potential cultural trends before they happen. If the potential cultural trend is a positive one for the organization, then we can plan in advance to maximize its positive impact. If the potential cultural trend is a negative one for the organization, then we can institute a damage control plan well in advance of the impact.

Once a potential cultural change agent is identified, the leaders of the organization should estimate its probability for causing either positive or negative change in the organization. Initially, this will have to be done based on executive logic and consensus. The executive making the initial estimate of the probability of a cultural agent change potential should also estimate the timing of the impact.

After the initial identification and potential impact have been accomplished, a data gathering should be undertaken by an identified individual or team to help refine the initial estimate of potential impact as well as the timing of the impact.

Initial organizations can use this as a historical tool to plot the effect of past change agents on the organization. This tool is an excellent adjunct to the purpose plot and cultural hierarchy.

The Future-Focused Organization

Those organizations that will not survive in the near future will be those that fail to change their core culture and principles, which served them well in a previous golden era, but are now outdated in the current fast moving and changing competitive environment. Figures 13a and b show some of the many parts that make up the core culture of an organization.

The migration to a future-focused organization is from left to right in the figures.

In future-focused organizations the purpose will define the culture required, instead of an ingrained culture defining a vision to support and further entrench its position. This will ensure that the omni pattern does not occur.

Scientific

Confused   (Decision making)   Purpose oriented

Participative

Hierarchical   (Organization)   Future focused

Two-way

Top down
and slow   (Information
transfer)   Interactive

Do and think

Just do   (Resource utilization)   Creative and valued
partners

(a)

Figure 4–13 (a)   Dimensions of Culture

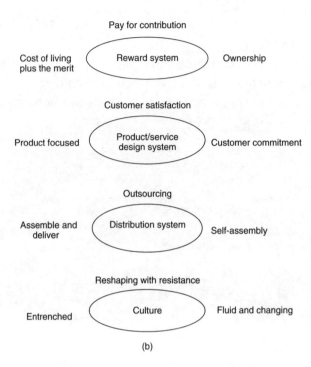

(b)

Figure 4–13 (b)   Dimensions of Culture

Competitive Analysis

A future-focused organization is managed for superior competitive advantage at all times in its areas of core competencies. Core competencies may change over time in a planned and timely manner to meet the needs of present and future customers. In a future-focused organization, changes in core competencies are done in a manner that does not cause the stressful environment in the organization that was described in Chapter 1.

Managing the business for competitive advantage requires the following of an organization:

- Realize that competitive success depends on building a cost or value advantage into one's product or service and then beating competitors to the marketplace.
- Excel at product and/or market definition.
- Manage the creative process to reduce the idea-to-market cycle time.
- Create better-designed business concepts, processes, and structure(s). This is accomplished through a thorough and rigorous management review process.

- Excel at managing the overall business system, including *internal* interrelationships within the company and *external* relationships with suppliers, customers, regulators, and competitors.
- Focus on customer commitment as a partnership arrangement and let the competition concentrate on customer satisfaction.
- Continue to pursue performance improvement in all aspects of the business by focusing on any or all of the following:

  ✘ Better functional execution within the business system

  ✘ Fine-tune interfaces between functional areas

  ✘ Redesign or reengineer the entire business system

This process of competitive analysis is part of the process of helping the organization to accept and view change as an opportunity to be embraced and exploited for the advantage of all in the organization.

Future-focused organizations view change as opportunity and not as an unsettling problem. Change provides the potential for creativity and innovation. Innovation is viewed throughout the organization as the way to obtain the following desired results:

- Continuous controlled experimentation
- Obsession with understanding and meeting customer's needs
- Strong, supportive culture
- Looseness in idea-generation stage
- Disciplined assessment of the ideas in terms of commercial viability

This process helps management shape the overall organization to be constantly evaluating itself against present and future competitors and to keep the organization on a path of innovation and self-renewal of its core competencies.

Future-focused organizations shape the overall organization to be innovative and self-renewing since management understands that just doing better is not adequate for preeminent performance. Preeminent performance requires an organization to make quantum improvements every 2 to 3 years. These quantum improvements must be planned, orchestrated, and focused on attaining a significant position in an existing or emerging market segment.

Future-focused organizations realize that quantum leaps involving major changes are more valuable than pursuing incremental improvements. Incremental improvements, while important, take time to amount to a significant change. Quantum improvements involves a major change in the organization and the way it conducts business.

Management in a future-focused organization leads by designing organizations and management processes that look forward and look out. Future-focused organizations do not want a culture that is satisfied with preserving the status quo but one that prefers to continually look for next steps, that is, self-renewal and the solution-after-next.[1] Future-focused organizations exploit opportunities that arise internally, as well as effectively using the forces at work in the external environment to their own advantage.

The process of market and competitive analysis will be necessary as we enter the 21st century. This type of analysis has been a strategic imperative of the 1990s but one that has not

---

1. G. Hoffherr, J. Moran, and G. Nadler, *Breakthrough Thinking in Total Quality Management,* Prentice Hall PTR, Englewood Cliffs, N.J., 1994, pp. 49–50.

been well exploited. Future-focused organizations are going to exist in a turbulent 21st century characterized by the following:

- Slower growth
- Lower profit margins
- Gridlocked government; difficult to get cooperative business legislation passed to be able to compete with other countries
- Intense global competition; price competition will be the norm
- Bankrupt social programs: federal, state, and local government
- Higher taxation to pay for the bankrupt government programs
- More unprepared and unskilled high school and college students entering the work force
- Burgeoning automation
- Rapid obsolescence due to technological change
- Deregulation and reregulation
- Information overload
- Instability in raw material prices
- Selective economic destabilization
- Major changes in macroeconomics and sociopolitical systems
- Lots of questions and uncertainty

Management in a future-focused organization must use the competitive analysis process to achieve the following:

- Define the business in which it wishes to be a leader and not an imitator. Imitation will lead to problems, since the rapid pace of change will quickly render obsolete what is being imitated.

- Focus the scarce resources of the organization in a manner that is more efficient and effective than the competition's. The leader must eliminate marginal and nonvalued activities.

- Focus on building a profitable long-term business that reinvests constantly in key competitive strengths and its employees.

- Constantly surprise the marketplace with innovative and unique value-added products that the competition can at best imitate.

- Focus on customer commitment and their needs while keeping the competition confused.

This process involves a shift in management that customarily uses some or all of the following strategies to outperform the competition:

- Cost leadership
- Differentiation
- Unique product and/or services
- Selective focus segmentation
- Geographic focus

A future-focused organization analyzes its competition now and in the future. Looking for potential new entrants and assessing the threat of that new entrant is a major undertaking for a future-focused organization. This requires the allocation of resources that will function as an intelligence agency by constantly monitoring trends in the environment that we compete in to give the organization the earliest possible warning signal, thus allowing us to react quickly. On the plus side in this environment is that a future-focused organization can help shape the environment by focusing on expanding current and future customer expectations with a steady stream of new, innovative, and value added products and services.

Competitive analysis must also focus on the threat of substitutes and not just direct competition. Substitute competition, especially in telecommunication, electronics, and media, is one that must be monitored closely.

Every future-focused organization must have a competitive intelligence agency that is focused on depicting trends, but also on analyzing the forces or root causes for the change that is coming about. They must clearly understand and assess the risks involved in any reaction to trends uncovered and reported. They must give an initial estimate of the type and amount of skills required, capital to be invested, other resources required, and the payback to pursue the changes uncovered.

As new trends emerge, a future-focused organization must constantly be asking itself how it should be organized to adequately respond in a timely manner to exploit any emerging opportunity to its fullest advantage.

Competitive Analysis Evaluation Process

The following competitive analysis evaluation process has been designed to provide an organization with an objective analysis of how its products or services compare with current major competitors and potential future entrants into the marketplace.

Competitive analysis is one tool that helps the leadership of a future-focused organization to understand its ability and capacity to respond to opportunities in a rapidly changing global marketplace. The ability to respond quickly to the marketplace is one critical indicator of an organization's health.

This process helps an organization identify organizational performance gaps that are both positive and negative. This process assists an organization in planning changes and modifications to its product and service lines. This leads to long-term market advantages and position.

It is recommended that the competitive analysis evaluation of a product or service line be completed by a lateral management team that is collectively familiar with all details of the line under analysis.

Another use for this process is to enhance and verify any quality function deployment[2] (QFD) or concurrent engineering[3] (CE) studies that may be undertaken on the product or service line under analysis in the future.

The purpose of this competitive evaluation process is to analyze the marketplace to determine what the industry we are in will look like in the future. A 3- or 5-year or longer time frame for the analysis should be used. Our goal is to determine which firms will be the most successful in the future and why. Once we understand the reasons why, we can then mobilize our organizational resources to be the most successful firm. We also want to estimate if and by how much the competition will intensify, as well as the opportunities and threats that we will face in the future.

Four forms will help an organization to complete a competitive evaluation process:

- Form A: Market Scope
- Form B: Customer Satisfaction Analysis

2. J. Moran, S. Marsh, S. Nakui, and G. Hoffherr, *Training and Facilitating in Quality Function Deployment,* GOAL/QPC, Methuen, Mass., 1991.
3. S. Shina, *Concurrent Engineering and Design of Electronic Products,* Van Nostrand Reinhold, N.Y., 1991.

- Form C: Criteria Comparison
- Form D: Competitive Comparison Summary

The forms and instructions on how to use them follow.

Form A: Market Scope

Form A should be filled out for each major product line or service provided by the organization as follows:

A. Identify the product or service.

B. Define the market size in dollars now and the potential in 3 years.

C. Identify the organization's current market share in percentage now and the potential in 3 years (if the current business plan is followed).

D. Define the profitability now and the potential in 3 years.

E. Identify the top three competitors and their market share percentage now and an estimate of their market share in 3 years.

F. Scan the horizon and identify potential new entrants into the market. For each potential new entrant, estimate their effect on the market now and in 3 years. The effect may be an expansion of the market, increase or reduction in the market share, elimination of a major competitor, and so on. A definitive definition of the threat of new entrants should be summarized in this step.

G. Identify who are the profitable and cost-effective competitors in the marketplace and why. Identify possible unique strategies being used that could be copied or improved on.

Form A: Market Scope

Competitive Analysis Self-evaluation Process

A. Identify the product or
   service : _____

	Now	3 Years
B. Market size	$ _____	$ _____
C. Our market share	_____%	_____%
D. Profitability $ and %	_____	_____

E.   Current top competitors   Market share percentage

	Now	3 Years
1. _____	_____%	_____%
2. _____	_____%	_____%
3. _____	_____%	_____%

F.   Potential new entrants   Effect on the market

	Now	3 Years
1. _____	_____	_____
2. _____	_____	_____
3. _____	_____	_____

G. Identify the most profitable cost-effective
   producer(s) and the reasons why:

   Potential threat summary:

H. Do we continue with this product or service? (Reasons)

H. Based on the preceding analysis, determine whether
    this product or service line should continue to be
    offered in the future.

Form B: Customer Satisfaction Analysis

This part of the process starts with the competitive lateral management evaluation team brainstorming a potential list of evaluation criteria. Once the list is developed, the evaluation

Form B: Customer Satisfaction

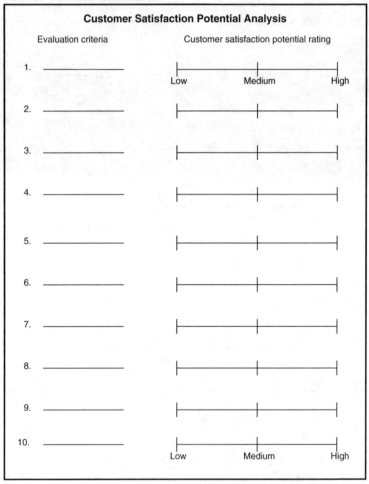

team should prioritize the list into the top eight to ten criteria. Criteria selected should be ones that have a high customer satisfaction potential. The facilitator or team leader could use Form B to facilitate this process selection. Each of the criteria chosen should have a separate Form C filled out for it.

Here is a potential list of evaluation criteria:

- Product performance
- Durability
- Serviceability
- Availability
- Features
- Ease of use
- Controls
- Price
- Cost
- Environmental
- Shape
- Performance parameters
- Reliability
- Functionality

Form C: Criteria Comparisons

Each of the criteria being used by the lateral management evaluation team to evaluate the product or service under consideration should have a Form C filled out for it.

1. Identify the product or service being evaluated.
2. List the evaluation criteria: identify in as much detail as possible. Some evaluation criteria that an evaluation team might utilize follow Form C:

Form C: Criteria Comparison

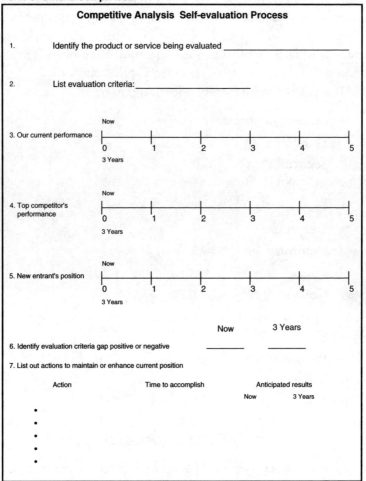

Competitive Analysis Self-evaluation Process

1.   Identify the product or service being evaluated _____

2.   List evaluation criteria:_____

3. Our current performance
Now
0   1   2   3   4   5
3 Years

4. Top competitor's performance
Now
0   1   2   3   4   5
3 Years

5. New entrant's position
Now
0   1   2   3   4   5
3 Years

                                      Now   3 Years

6. Identify evaluation criteria gap positive or negative   _____   _____

7. List out actions to maintain or enhance current position

Action	Time to accomplish	Anticipated results	
		Now	3 Years
•			
•			
•			
•			
•			

✘   Product performance

✘   Durability

✘   Serviceability

✘   Availability

- ✗ Features
- ✗ Ease of use
- ✗ Controls
- ✗ Price
- ✗ Cost
- ✗ Environmental
- ✗ Shape
- ✗ Performance parameters
- ✗ Reliability
- ✗ Functionality

3. On a scale of 0 (nothing) to 5 (world class) rate the organization's identified product or service as to its current performance against the criteria under consideration on the top of the scale. On the bottom of the scale, rate where the product or service performance will be in 3 years if the current business plan is followed.

4. Rate the top competitor(s)'s competing product or service the same as in step 3.

5. Scan the horizon and rate any potential new entrant's competitive performance the same as in step 3.

6. Identify the performance gap for this evaluation criteria as either positive (market leader) or negative (market lagger) currently and in 3 years. The organization should document reasons for the gap in as much detail as necessary to help with the action planning section.

7. In this part of Form C the evaluation team would develop specific actions that could be taken to maintain or enhance the current or future market position

of the product or service under evaluation. For each action identified, the evaluation team needs to (1) estimate the time it will take to accomplish the action recommended and (2) anticipate the results from the action now and in 3 years.

Before any actions are initiated, all the actions from each of the evaluation criteria should be compared to each other to determine if any of them are supportive of each other or if there is a negative interaction or conflict that could be a problem later in the design or redesign process. Negative interac-

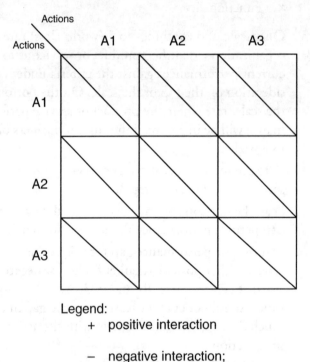

Figure 5.1   L-Shaped Matrix

tions should be highlighted and investigated to eliminate the problem before the action is initiated. This comparison can be accomplished using an L-shaped matrix as shown in Figure 5.1. This matrix analysis will help the evaluation team to determine if any actions are supportive of or in conflict with each other.

The prioritization matrix shown in Figure 5.2 can be used to help rank order the actions and the allocation of resources.

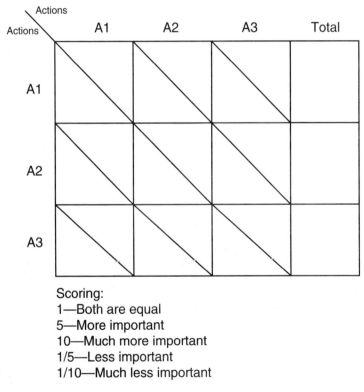

Figure 5.2 Prioritization Matrix

Form D: Competitive Comparison Summary

Form D can be used to capture the results of the entire evaluation of a product or service. This form shows the favorable or unfavorable gaps for all the criteria used in the competitive analysis self-evaluation process.

Form D: Competitive Position

Competitive Comparison Summary

Product or service evaluated: _____

Evaluation criteria   Competitive gap comparision

                                    Unfavorable   Favorable

1. _____ |——————|——————|——————|——————|
                           -5   -3   0   +3   +5

2. _____ |——————|——————|——————|——————|

3. _____ |——————|——————|——————|——————|

4. _____ |——————|——————|——————|——————|

5. _____ |——————|——————|——————|——————|

6. _____ |——————|——————|——————|——————|

7. _____ |——————|——————|——————|——————|

8. _____ |——————|——————|——————|——————|
                           -5   -3   0   +3   +5

Summary

These forms will help a future-focused organization develop a risk profile of the future. This risk profile will be an input into the strategic plan, which will help with the investment, resource, and organizational decisions that will make a future-focused organization the constant market leader.

A future-focused organization uses its market intelligence to seize the high market ground by concentrating its resources to obtain superiority in specific high-return markets, to surprise and keep the competition off balance by constant innovation, and to continually reinvest in its key competitive strengths. Once a future-focused organization achieves superiority, it does not let it competitors recover.

Future-Focused Organizational Planning Process

The path to becoming a future-focused organization is to develop a long-term strategic plan, deploy it to your organization, allow them to respond with specific short-term strategies to achieve it, review and negotiate measures of success with them on each strategy, monitor progress, provide an uninterrupted two-way flow of communications, constantly focus on simplifying daily work and reducing waste, and constantly monitor the environment you are dealing with. This is complete organizational alignment. The strategic plan must be a living document that facilitates organizational decision making.

Sounds simple enough, but very few organizations have been successful in accomplishing this. Unfortunately, most strategic planning and deployment activities of organizations are full of good intentions, but lack a determination and commitment to properly execute them. They usually contain impossible and escalating expectations that are thoroughly documented and then put away on a shelf in the top executives' bookcases until they are dusted off for the next year's update.

The future-focused organization's strategic planning process described in this chapter is results bound and not bookshelf bound. In a future-focused organization, strategic planning is not an event, occurring once per year with great fanfare, but rather an ongoing process occurring every day.

The importance of strategic planning in the near future was stated in the International Quality Study,[1] which showed "that all countries studied are increasing their emphasis on considering customer satisfaction in their strategic planning process, but Japan has a considerable lead over Germany and the United States. Although this lead will be reduced during the next three years, the gap will not be eliminated. *This is a significant business advantage for Japan.*"

If the strategic planning process is done correctly, it helps shape how the organization approaches its daily work in a way that is aligned with the long-term goals of the organization.

The future-focused organization's strategic planning process is shown in an overview in Figure 6-1. The tools or techniques mentioned in each step are discussed in other chapters in more detail (refer to the index).

This process starts with a look in the corporate mirror, as shown in step 1 of Figures 6.1 and 6.2. We may like the image we see or we may not. The purpose of looking in the corporate mirror is not just to see the image but to understand in detail why the image exists and how it projects itself. We want to examine the internal and external molecules of the image. We accomplish this in step 1 of Figures 6.1 and 6.2. A thorough assessment of the internal environment or operating climate

---

1. H. James Harrington, Beyond Blind Faith, *European Quality,* June 1993, pp. 60–67.

Step 1: Unlocking the Corporate Information Reservoir	Step 2: Business Purpose Document and Understand Current Corporate Position
• Assessment • Strategic business information • Information relevance • Gap Analysis • Identification of information for future-focused organization • Reduction of information waste • Internal/external analysis	• Use input from step 1 • Purpose hierarchy • Purpose plot • Market field location • Customer response matrix • Cultural hierarchy • Technology hierarchy • Internal/external benchmarking

Step 3: Purpose Gap Exploration	Step 4: Integrated Business Plan

• Document purpose gap
• Purpose gap matrix
• Input from steps 1 and 2
  • Financial analysis
  • Market plan
  • Competitor analysis
  • Financial plan
  • Product/service development plan
	• What has to be accomplished
	• Long-term goals (3 to 5 years)
	• Short-term targets (1-year objectives)
	• Integrated focus
	• Alignment of plans
	• Rough schedules
	• Prioritization of resources
	• Where the organization is going
	• Clarity of purpose

Step 5: How to Achieve the Plan	Step 6: Concurrent Exploration
• Identify the critical purpose factors to close the 3- to 5-year gap • Build agreement and consensus • Broad statements of intent • Details to be developed in step 6	• Identify critical systems and results-oriented goals • Identify critical cultural philosophies and activity-oriented goals • Develop strategies and identify key strategies • Align where necessary

Step 7: Strategy Analysis and Trade-off	Step 8: Organizational Impact Analysis
• Criteria matrix • Costs versus accomplishments • Information collection objectives identified	• Environmental scan • Transitional time line • Implementation analysis

Step 9: Future-Focused Organization	Step 10: Results Management
• Solution-after-next • Betterment timeline • Cultural timeline	• 80/20 reviews • What to review • Review timing

Step 11: Standardize
• Reengineering • Institute daily management • Eliminate wasteful and noncritical operations

Figure 6.1   Future-Focused Organization Strategic Planning Model for Complete Organizational Alignment

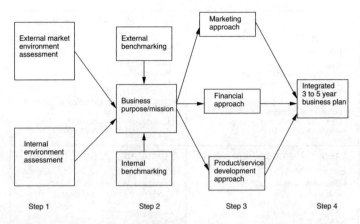

Figure 6.2   Future-Focused Organization Strategic Planning Model
for Complete Organizational Alignment

plus the external environment and marketplace is conducted.
The organization unlocks its corporate information reservoir
and focuses on the information that is needed to do this assessment. The information reservoir needs to be updated on a regular basis to adequately track the external and internal
environment and prepare for change. Figure 6.3 shows the
possible data that may be relevant in this assessment step. Not
all the categories apply to every organization. Some of these
data already exist in various parts of the organization and need
to be pulled together. Because of the functional barriers that
exist in organizations, needed data are not shared. Some of the
assessment data may need to be researched and analyzed by an
internal or external source. All the pertinent assessment data
should be assembled into a fact book. This fact book should be
considered the main reference document and be distributed to
the members of the senior executive team that will be doing
the strategic planning. This type of strategic planning fact
book can be assembled in a month's time by a high-level staff

Assessment data	Substantiation		Relevance			Source document and date of issue
	Fact based	Opinion based	Low	Medium	High	
1. Employee satisfaction						
2. Mission/Vision statements						
3. Current strategy						
4. Current 5-year plan						
5. Financial data						
6. Customer retention						
7. Customer complaints						
8. Referred business						
9. Returned products						
10. Competitive rankings						
11. Performance against customer standards/needs						
12. Customer loyalty						
13. Customer commendations						
14. Product/services measures						
15. Process measures						
16. Industry evaluations						
17. Community relations						
18. Regulatory compliance						
19. Vendor data						
20. Awards/recognitions						
21. Self-assessments (Baldrige/ISO)						
22. Shareholder measures						
23. Foreign competition						
24. Economic cycles						
25. Demographic changes						
26. Other						

Figure 6.3 Assessment Data Evaluation

person. Once the fact book is developed and assembled, a careful assessment as to the relevance of the data regularly collected should be completed. The BreakThrough Thinking®[2] principle of *limited information collection* should be applied and adhered to.

---

2. G. Hoffherr, J. Moran, and G. Nadler, *Breakthrough Thinking in Total Quality Management*, Prentice Hall PTR, Englewood Cliffs, N.J., 1994.

After imaging, the next step (step 2 of Figures 6.1 and 6.2) is to develop the purpose of the organization today. The purpose of the organization is similar to its mission, and the senior executive team needs to carefully evaluate where the organization is today and where it should be in the future based on the data in the fact book and not just their own selfish ambition. Purpose focuses in on why the organization exists. Purpose is similar to mission; what is the business that the organization is in or will be in and how they are going to get there? The purpose of an organization is a very definitive short statement void of modifiers.[3]

Here are some examples of purpose statements:

- Chemical company: To produce, package, and ship fine chemicals.
- Rehabilitation hospital: To provide inpatient rehabilitation services in the metro west market.
- Agricultural company: To support suppliers and service business segments.
- Armed Forces: To safeguard our nation's territories.
- Pharmaceutical company: To discover, manufacture, and sell prescription and over-the-counter drugs.

In each statement there are no listings of many of the major modifiers that are seen in vision statements, such as customer focus, high quality, people participation, empowerment, and so on. These modifiers are understood as part of the infrastructure of a future-focused organization. Many organizations have spent years of people labor writing and rewriting vision statements. One of the authors was once the chairperson of a vision development task force of a fortune 500 company. This

---

3. Ibid.

vision development process lasted 8 months, meetings were every Friday for 4 hours, and the vision task force had eight senior managers as team members in addition to a trained facilitator. The chairperson also met once per month with the president and senior vice-presidents for 2 hours to review progress. By now you have developed a mental tally of the costs involved. Can you draw any similarities to your organization?

After 9 months a two-page vision statement was developed and approved. The insight the author gained through this experience was that the vision was not related to the purpose of the organization. The corporate songwriters had added enough modifiers so that their functions were justified in the future. The vision was built on the capabilities of the current leaders. A few years later this organization missed major shifts in their market that caused a loss of market share, which led to financial problems.

To save future vision writers 8 or more months of agony a *generic vision statement process* has been developed and is shown in Figure 6.4.

Future-focused organizations focus on their purpose and not the vision. The purpose hierarchy, once it is defined for the organization today, is then expanded into a hierarchy of exceedingly more ambitious achievements. Usually five to eight purposes are developed for the hierarchy. The organization then focuses on the one purpose in the hierarchy that they feel they can achieve in the next 3 to 4 years.

The agricultural company mentioned previously might have picked from their hierarchy *To have an integrated food and agricultural company.* The rehabilitation hospital might have picked *To provide rehabilitation services not only to inpatients but to outpatients.* Each organization would pick a higher-level

We will be a better organization tomorrow than we are today. This will be accomplished by focusing on (pick any two of the following)

- Total quality management
- SPC
- JIT
- MRP
- Continuous improvement
- Customer satisfaction
- Employee involvement
- Teamwork

Top management will personally lead this future-focused organization by (pick any two of the following):

- Benchmarking the best in class
- Visibility
- Develop and project quality values
- Data-driven decisions
- Standardize our processes
- Make long-term decisions

Our employees, who are our most important asset, will (pick any two of the following):

- Share in the rewards of the superior performance
- Have increased job pride
- Develop new salable skills
- Feel empowered
- Be part of the planning process
- Be recognized for their contribution

This will be accomplished in a collaborative atmosphere, with respect for each other and a true valuing of the differing perceptions of others. We will continually strive to (pick any two of the following):

- Meet or exceed the needs of our customer
- Meet the needs of our work force
- Meet the needs of our investors
- Improve our performance to be in alignment with customer expectations
- Develop cooperative partnerships with our suppliers
- Develop innovative products that are delivered quickly to the market

Our future-focused organization will have a social focus that will be an inspiration to the rest of our (pick any two of the following):

- Industry
- Clients
- Suppliers
- Community
- Country
- World
- Universe

We will be the industry benchmark leader in the 21st century.

Figure 6.4 Generic Vision Statement

purpose from their hierarchy to focus on and achieve over the next 3 to 4 years.

Some of the tools that senior executives in a future-focused organization can use to help them in developing their organization's purpose are the following:

- Purpose hierarchy
- Purpose plot
- Market field location
- Present and potential customer response matrix
- Cultural hierarchy
- Technology hierarchy

Once the higher-level purpose is picked, the senior executive team undertaking this planning process would then develop the purpose gap. The purpose gap is a process to help the senior executives fully understand how far away they are from their future purpose. This purpose gap is a multidimensional analysis on a number of factors. This analysis is accomplished by utilizing a visual graphic such as a radar chart. The factors identified for the purpose gap analysis are first rated for the organization today by the senior executive planning team. Once this analysis is done and plotted, a similar comparison can be made for the organization's major competitor. Once the results of this analysis are plotted, it can be overlaid on the organization's rating. Positive and negative gaps will be obvious to the senior executive planning team. Negative gaps should cause a sense of urgency in the team and develop the desire to move forward to surpass the competition in the near future.

Once the purpose of the organization is established the next step, as shown in Figures 6.1 and 6.2, is to develop the marketing, financial, and product/service development approaches required to attain the purpose that the organization is striving for.

The marketing field location tool is one that is useful in determining the strengths and weaknesses of the organization's existing products as compared to the competition. The development of the marketing approach should define the markets that the organization will be in or entering and the markets that they will not compete in and provide a broad outline of how they will accomplish this. The marketing approach should set the broad context of how the organization intends to achieve its purpose. It will define *where* the organization will be focusing its efforts to establish and build a loyal customer base.

The financial approach documents the revenue, profit, and capital needs of the organization to achieve its stated purpose. The financial approach is a broad outline of *what* must happen for the organization to be successful. The financial approach should consider all the potential financial possibilities available to the organization to achieve the defined revenue, profit, and capital needs. The strengths and weaknesses of each financial possibility should be detailed and prioritized.

The product/service development approach should outline the *need* for new or enhanced products and services that will occur and the potential timeline for their development or acquisition. The technology hierarchy is a tool that may be of help to the developers of the product/service development approach since it shows the type of technology that will be needed to meet the timeline. The product/service development approach shows what existing products will be used, what enhancements will be required, and what development or acquisition efforts will be required and when.

At any point in steps 1 through 3 of Figure 6.2 a process known as *catchball* can be deployed in the organization to get other points of view and inputs. This catchball process is usually accomplished by having the members of the senior executive planning team each conduct a few focus groups of eight to ten people in the organization at various levels to share and get reactions from the current output of a particular step. The purpose of this catchball process is not only to get input, but also to start to develop widespread ownership in the organization's future direction. The senior executive conducting the catchball session presents the output that he or she wants feedback on. The discussion can be enhanced by having a facilitator present to help keep the discussion and feedback focused. The output of a catchball session should be a document that lists the groups agreements, areas that require additional clarification, disagreements, and recommendations. The form shown in Figure 6.5 could be used to document each catchball session.

Catchball Rules:

- Do it live and in person rather than by mail or phone; the interaction and ability to clarify in real time with the attendees is important.

- Do it in small groups, eight to ten, and allow these people to discuss it, not the senior management team representative.

- Focus the discussion to the output(s) assigned to the group; use the catchball form (Figure 6.5) to help with the focus.

- Do not be defensive of the output(s) under discussion; practice active listening and do not interrupt. A new management skill set that may have to be learned.

- Record all the comments in the appropriate area on the catchball form.

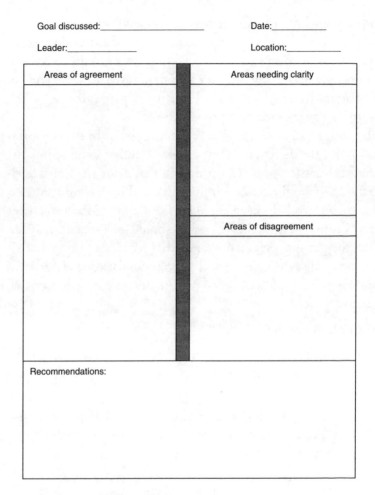

Figure 6.5   Catchball Form

- Allow about 15 to 30 minutes per section on the form; you want to capture the main points and initial reactions.

- Summarize all the feedback on each output on one catchball sheet.

- Schedule a management team meeting to discuss the feedback and make changes where appropriate. Document why feedback was not used.
- Present the original output in the revised form to the original catchball groups and discuss why the feedback was not incorporated; close the loop.
- The senior management planning team makes the ultimate decisions with guidance from the catchball sessions.

Figure 6.6 is a summary form for the catchball process to give the catchball groups a sense of management's intent toward a particular goal. Once the goals are finalized, this form should be filled out for each goal and distributed or published throughout the organization.

Once the catchball process and the revised marketing, financial, and product/service approach revisions have been completed, the senior executive planning group must now craft an integrated 3- to 5-year business plan that delineates *what has to be accomplished* and *when*. Goals are set that must be achieved, and once these goals are defined the catchball process could again be used. The more the catchball process is used, the more widespread ownership to the strategic plans becomes and the more likely they will be achieved.

The integrated business plan will define in broad terms the key result areas, performance indicators, and overall budget allocations. Figure 6.7 shows a conceptual framework for the plan that will drive the budget.

Now the integrated business plan must be turned into a results management process. This results management process focuses the organization as a whole on steps 5 through 11 as shown in Figure 6.1. Steps 5 through 11 are a deployment and review process that lets the rest of the organization internalize the integrated business plan and determine their functional

Goal:_____   Time frame:_____

Meaning:

How will we measure it?

What will be the impact on our organization?

    • 1 year

    • 3 years

Estimated impact on customers:

Estimated impact on employees:

Estimated impact on shareholders:

What is senior management's role?

Figure 6.6   Goal Statement Form

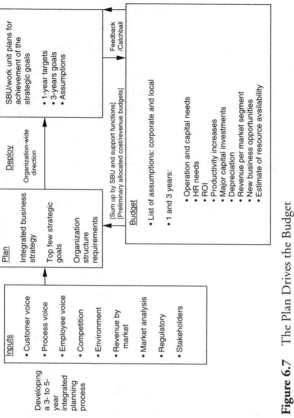

Figure 6.7 The Plan Drives the Budget

contributions and how they will accomplish the contributions identified. The senior executive planning team should also follow steps 5 through 11 at their level to focus on the projects they should undertake organization wide. Some of these senior executive projects can be deployed to lateral teams, and some are the sole domain of the senior executives. These senior executives projects are usually focused on removing major obstacles that impede lateral, business unit, and daily management improvement teams from effectively accomplishing needed change. The focus in the remainder of this chapter is on the deployment process to functional business units, but the process is similar for the senior executive planning team.

The first step for a business unit functional team is to define the critical purpose factors that must be achieved in order to close the gap between what they need to do and what must be achieved. Critical purpose factors are a combination of operational and cultural change factors that must occur for agreed upon contributions to be achieved. These critical purpose factors focus a functional business unit on what has to be achieved over the next 3 to 5 years. They can be reviewed and modified on a yearly basis if any external conditions change drastically, either positively or negatively. To develop these critical purpose factors, an affinity and prioritization process is used. These two processes are explained in Chapter 7.

Critical purpose factors are defined as follows:

- Items that need to be different in the future from today

- Ways to run the business unit to achieve its purpose

- They cover all aspects of the business

- Usually have five to eight (the fewer the better) critical purpose factors

- Items that can be deployed throughout the business unit and not just the domain of management

- Broad achievement possibilities

Critical purpose factors can be divided into two types as follows:

1. *Operational goals:* The "whats," or things to keep us going and growing with a focus on our customer.

2. *Cultural Goals: The "hows,"* or ways to behave (values), interact (cooperate), encourage (reward and recognize), and make decisions (thought process).

More specific examples of operational and cultural goals are the following:

Critical operational factors: growth, speed, delivery, cost reduction, productivity increases, revenue growth, increase value added, customer satisfaction, market and growth, manage the business, grow the business, safety, environmental, technology, community relations, sales mix, return on capital employed

- Assure manufacturing capabilities and capacities
- Develop a technology management strategy
- Worldwide sourcing
- Assure regulatory compliance
- Focus product, streamline strategies
- Reengineer critical business processes
- Improve R&D productivity
- Manage product life cycles; saying no to customers you cannot satisfy
- Manage environmental and competitive trends
- Vigorously pursue the total satisfaction of every customer
- Exceed every yearly profit and cash flow commitment
- Aggressively increase the organization's value through profitable growth in customers, products, and new businesses
- Pursue relentlessly operating cost reduction
- Demonstrate capability for effective cost management
- Achievement of $XXX or % gain in revenue

- Continuation of earnings record or X% increase/year
- 10% Growth in traditional businesses and a 20% growth in new businesses
- Develop distinct competencies in R&D
- Strive to exceed yearly profit and cash flow commitments
- Aggressively increase shareholder value
- Institute benchmark safety and environmental practices
- Relentless pursuit of continuous improvement and cost reduction
- Small business units will have a positive economic value added
- Aggressively manage product life cycles
- Typical return on investment and return on assets financial goals
- Achieve a 90% reduction in our most critical errors in products, processes, and services in 3 years
- Out of the box quality of new goods and services will meet customer requirements and will be equal to or better than the competitors
- Delivery goal: 100% on time
- 5% Reduction in personal injuries
- ISO 9000 certification by 19xx
- Facility goals

Critical cultural factors: **management by fact, build teams/teamwork, employee satisfaction, empowerment, work-force management**

- Optimization of the human dimensions of the business
- Define the desired culture and values
- Encourage and reward cross-functional interactions

- Train and educate for superior competitive performance
- Develop strategies to retain key people
- Satisfy every employee by providing challenging and rewarding work
- Ensure that every employee possesses the skills and knowledge to succeed
- Full integration of the quality concepts into our business processes
- Complete adherence to our company values
- Open, honest, and timely communication will be the norm
- Increase employee training for meeting job requirements to an average of 5% of time worked
- Attendance goals
- Participation in 401k-type programs
- Improved and expanded education programs
- Employee customer visit programs

The critical purpose factors, once identified, are then deployed within the business units. The deployment process allows the business units to respond as to how they will contribute to the overall accomplishment that was identified in step 6 of Figure 6.1. During this part of the process, the critical business systems and processes are identified. Goals are then developed for these critical business systems and processes. Strategies are designed and approved to accomplish these goals. This process is shown in Figure 6.8.

Once the strategies and actions have been developed and aligned, they need to be detailed out to the specifics as described in step 7 of Figure 6.1. The use of a *SMART matrix* is recommended for this step. Figure 6.9 shows the SMART

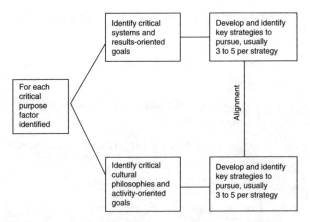

Figure 6.8 Concurrent Exploration

matrix concept. The use of this matrix helps the management team to determine exactly what they want accomplished, how they will measure these accomplishments, who will be responsible for the specifics, and the resources required (people, dollars, space, equipment, and so on). Management will prioritize and make rational trade-offs when the resources required are more than available. The trade-offs will allow the scope of the project to be changed or adjusted. The SMART matrix forces a logical discussion on desired cost versus accomplishments trade-offs. This is an important step in which scarce resources are focused and deployed for maximum results.

The management of the business units needs to keep a focus in step 8 of Figure 6.1 on the following three areas:

1. Environment in which they operate

2. Transition into change

3. Implementation of change

The environment in which the improvements or change will take place needs to be monitored on a regular basis to

Specifics	Measures	Accountable	Resources	Time

Figure 6.9 SMART Matrix

ensure that improvement teams operate successfully. The business unit management as well as the senior executive planning team need to use the *environmental scan process* to understand what might go wrong and how to plan for contingencies. The main objective of the environmental scan process is to ensure that improvement efforts are successful and do not get bogged down in obstacles that were unforeseen or not planned for. Figure 6.10 shows the environmental scan form. The matrix is divided into two parts. The right-hand side deals with the neg-

How	Why	Positive	Negative	Why	How

Force strength   H M L   L M H

Figure 6.10 Environmental Scan Form

ative forces affecting the process of change. Each negative force identified is rated as to the strength of the force: high, medium, or low. The high and medium forces are further analyzed as to why they occur. Once we understand why the negative force occurs, we can then develop contingencies, "hows," to either overcome it or neutralize its effect. The left-hand side of the matrix deals with the positive and proactive influencers that can make the project successful. The positive forces can be analyzed as to why they occur and how to increase their strength. The senior management planning team needs to determine how to use these forces to leverage against the negative forces that exist in the environment that they are dealing with.

The environmental scan matrix needs to be reviewed on a regular basis, every 3 to 6 months, to adequately monitor a changing environment and to continue to ensure the success of the project teams that may have been commissioned.

The next part of this step is to develop a *transitional timeline*[4] as shown in Figure 6.11. The transitional timeline helps a

---

4. Ibid., p 356.

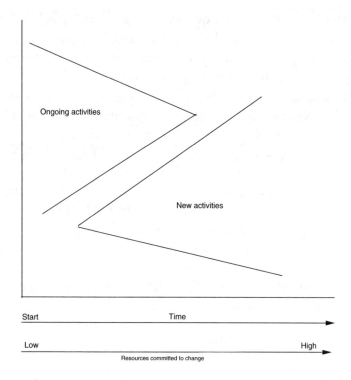

Start

Time

Low   High

Resources committed to change

Figure 6.11 Transitional Timeline

planning or improvement team to identify which activities should be eliminated or reengineered and when. It also helps us to identify when activities are improved or eliminated and what type of resources will be freed up and available for redeployment to further speed up the change and improvement. The transitional timeline also indicates when new activities are to be added. The main idea of the transitional timeline is to focus an organization on the fact that change can be planned and that to leave it to chance is to invite a disaster. Too often we see a change get implemented with half of the old system and half of the new system in place. This situation produces more stress and strain in the organization and is frequently what happens when organizations have poorly implemented programs, such as total quality management, material requirements planning, just in time, and others.

The senior executive planning team's work is not done once the deployment starts. At this point they begin to function like a future-focused organization leadership team and focus on step 9 of the planning model, as shown in Figure 6.1. In this step the senior executive planning team focuses on the future changes that the organization will require in order to maintain their leadership market position. Figure 6.12 shows a three part matrix that focuses on future-focused change.

The senior executive planning team utilizes this matrix to develop change for the future of their organization based on the planning done to date. To do this future change planning, three concepts are utilized:

1. Solution-after-next[5]

2. Betterment timeline[6]

3. Cultural timeline

First the senior executive planning team fills out the matrix by listing the changes that are currently being implemented and brainstorming and prioritizing for each of them the solution-after-next. The solution-after-next to the current changes that are being implemented is the next logical steps or breakthroughs that the organization needs to take to remain the leader in its marketplace. Since these solutions-after-next are betterments to the current changes being implemented, they

---

5. G. Hoffherr, J. Moran, and G. Nadler, *Breakthrough Thinking in Total Quality Management,* Prentice Hall PTR, Englewood Cliffs, N.J., 1994.
6. Ibid.

Current changes being implemented	Solution-after-next	Betterment timeline	Cultural timeline
1.			
2.			
3.			
4.			
5.			

Figure 6.12 Future Change Matrix

sometimes supersede those changes. However, they often will need the infrastructure that the current change will put into place before the organization is ready and able to implement them. A betterment timeline must be estimated for when these solutions-after-next can be started, and then lateral or functional teams must be put into place to ensure that they happen. This is a leadership and communication process to ensure the organization that change will continue and that the next change is already being discussed and developed. This process sends a message to the organization that the status quo will not be tolerated in the turbulent and fast-changing environment in which the organization exists and competes. The cultural timeline estimates the impact on the organization that the solution-after-next will have and the skills and behavior that will be needed to fully implement these changes. The cultural timeline is an estimation technique to understand how fluid and flexible our culture and employees must be. It reinforces the fact that our work force must be fluid, flexible, and continuously learning.

The future-focused organization leadership team now focuses on step 10 of the planning model, as shown in Figure 6.1. In this step the senior executive planning team focuses on results management. Results management is a process of obtaining progress reports from the organization as to the status of the change that has been agreed upon and put in place throughout the organization. These reviews should be of the 80/20 variety. In an 80/20 review, 80% of the review is focused on the current status of the projects being implemented, and 20% of the review is focused on the future change that will be needed. These reviews are opportunities for the senior executive planning team to communicate their discussions and agreements that have been captured in the future change matrix shown in Figure 6.12. These reviews should also focus on deviations from the plan that could adversely affect the change required. Teams implementing change should report adverse deviations from schedules along with a corrective action plan to put the project back on schedule. These results management reviews are also an effective time to reward and recognize individual and team members for making the change required and for following a future-focused organization process. Every 6 months the senior executive planning team should review steps 1 through 6 of the future-focused organization strategic planning model shown in Figure 6.1 to ensure that the actions being taken are appropriate and on course. Also, this is the time to check to see if anything in the marketplace has shifted and needs to be reflected in the change plan. In this results management review process, particular attention should be directed to the progress of the lateral teams since they are dealing in the most unstructured part of the organization's environment. Lateral teams need extra attention at first, since this will be a major change in the operation of the organization. These lateral teams need to be monitored closely to ensure their effectiveness and efficiency.

Step 11 of the future-focused organization strategic planning model as shown in Figure 6.1 is focused more on the daily management functions of the organization. In this step the daily management functions check their daily work systems against the future needs of the organization and decide which processes are valued added to the future needs, which need reengineering, and which should be eliminated. The daily management functions would institute continuous improvement and daily management on those processes that add value to the change required and those that have been reengineered. The daily management functions need to make sure that the needed processes are standardized, controllable, and functioning consistently to deliver the products and services required by the organization's customers.

The future-focused organization strategic planning model helps to ensure complete organizational alignment and a strategy that is consistent with maintaining market leadership, and not a strategy based on the ambition of the leaders or the existing resources. Strategies are not leader focused or threat focused (force employees into a mode based on threats of lay-offs), maintaining fit (we have always been in this market), or reducing costs faster than the loss in market share. Strategy is developed to achieve the organization's future purpose and to delight the customers, and not for self-gratification of the organizational leaders.

Summary

The strategy planing process helps senior management to find the critical few very important elements to deploy throughout their organization that will achieve substantial results and cause real change that will benefit the organization as a whole, and not just one or two segments of it. This process gives senior management a methodology that helps to explain to the rest of the organization the rationale for the focus on the critical few items chosen. The rest of the organization can believe in this process because they can understand the rationale of the process that senior management has followed. They can see that it is based on a methodology that is sound and that builds consensus at every stage.

In addition, this process can also align projects that may be undertaken at any level in the organization based on the future-focused plan developed. Figure 6.13 details such an alignment system to tie together senior management, lateral management, and daily management projects.

The benefit ratio is the decision point on a particular project that has been suggested. This project is one of many that helps to focus the planned changed through the future-focused planning process. The benefit ratio is calculated by dividing the anticipated savings of pursuing the project by the anticipated costs that will be incurred. Examples of anticipated savings and costs are as follows:

Savings	Costs
☞ Increased market share	☞ Team time
☞ Reduction in defects	☞ Resources consumed
☞ Cost reduction	☞ People
☞ Cost avoidance	☞ Equipment
☞ Productivity gains	☞ Space
☞ Increase in revenue	☞ Supplies
☞ Reduced cycle time	☞ Systems development time
☞ Waste reduction	☞ Computer time
☞ Reduced inventory	☞ Computer capacity
☞ Opportunity cost avoidance	☞ Accelerated depreciation

If the benefit ratio is greater than 1, the project should be considered for action. The benefit ratios of the many suggested projects could be compared using a Pareto chart. From this comparison, the organization can choose to select only the highest benefit ratios to pursue.

Throughout this process the rest of the organization does not have to take a blind leap of faith every time change or a redirection is proposed. The rest of the organization can believe in change because it is focused and rational.

Senior Management Projects

Goal	Prioritized issues	System-wide improvement projects	Benefit ratio	Assigned to:

Lateral Management Projects

Company-wide goals	Short-term plans	Prioritized issues	Company-wide projects	Benefit ratio	Assigned to:

Daily Management Projects

Operational targets	Prioritized issues	Improvement projects	Benefit ratio	Assigned to:

Benefit ratio = anticipated savings/anticipated costs

Figure 6.13   Project Selection Criteria

Focusing and Expanding Customer Expectations

In our current economy many customers have needs that are not being met. These same customers also have needs that they have not recognized. How many electronic gadgets do you have today that you did not even think of one year ago? If you are like most of us, you have many that are now indispensable in your everyday life. It was only a short time ago that seeing a person using a personal computer on a plane was a rare sight; today it is common and such use is growing rapidly. These electronic gadgets have expanded our productivity since they have fulfilled a need we may not have recognized in the recent past. Our customer's life-style and culture are changing at a very fast pace. As this change takes place, many new needs will emerge that will have to be satisfied. New markets emerge rapidly and there will be a constantly changing competitive landscape.

Future-focused organizations are constantly focusing, anticipating, expanding, and redefining their customer's needs. Future-focused organizations deliver product bundles that help achieve the customer's purpose and directly contribute to customer success. Future-focused organizations do this by focusing on the trends that will influence and change their customer's culture and life-style. Changing culture and life-style generate new needs and expectations. If a future-focused organization can anticipate these cultural changes and have the product bundles available to service the emerging needs, it can dominate the market. This ability to anticipate and deliver value-adding product bundles in a timely fashion will help develop product loyalty and distinguish us from our competition. It is useless to anticipate the need and not be able to deliver. The future-focused organization's ability to anticipate cultural change affecting their customers allows it the opportunity to help customers to redefine their needs. The premise is that a future-focused organization does this to truly help their customers uncover or discover unrecognized or overlooked needs and then satisfies them profitably for both parties. This is not a bells and whistles adding process but one of providing true core value to the customer, which can then be used to expand the customer's ability to achieve its purpose in a timely and efficient manner.

Before a future-focused organization can begin the process of expanding and redefining their customer's expectations, it must first understand the current customer needs and where their organization fits in the overall marketplace. This a Baselining process that can be accomplished by utilizing two tools available to a future-focused organization.

Today, many organizations are laboring under a customer-driven planning model that causes them to be in a constant state of flux; this is an excellent example of the tail wagging the dog syndrome. Figure 7.1 shows a future-focused organization model that is mission, vision, and valued positioned and focused.

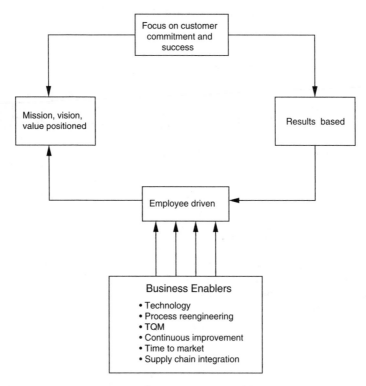

Figure 7.1   Future-Focused Organization Model

The first tool utilized in this process is the *market field location grid* shown in Figure 7.2. The market field location grid is used in conjunction with the Purpose Plot developed more fully in Chapter 10. The market field location grid is a graphic plot of where a particular organization fits into a well-defined or developing market or a combination of both types of markets. This tool provides the leaders of an organization with a visual consensus of the organization's current and/or planned place in the market that it has chosen to compete in.

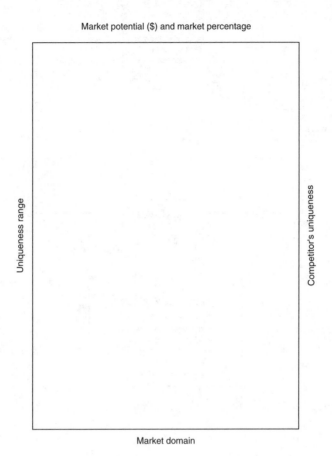

Figure 7.2   Market Field Location

The steps to construct the market field location grid are as follows:

   1. *Market domain:* The market domain is plotted on the bottom horizontal axis. The first step is to list all the current and potential market segments. Each segment is identified by a hash mark with the segment below it.

2. *Market potential* ($) and *market percentage:* Each segment identified on the bottom horizontal axis will ·have its market potential dollar volume and the organization's current percentage of that volume indicated above it on the top horizontal axis.

3. *Competitor's uniqueness:* On the right vertical axis we identify each of our major competitors and put an ✕ over each major market segment where they compete with us. Include their percentage of the current sales volume.

4. *Uniqueness range:* The uniqueness range is plotted on the left vertical axis. The first step is to list those factors (productivity service, organizational, and the like) that our organization possesses that are unique to us. These factors are listed individually on the left vertical axis, and a green oval is made over each market segment where the organization is fully exploiting this uniqueness. A red oval is made over each market segment where we are not exploiting this uniqueness. Blanks indicate no uniqueness and may be considered as market segments where the organization should no longer compete.

This visual graphic of the market field potential gives the designer of the organization of the future an indication of where the market strengths and weaknesses of the organization are today.

The next tool to be utilized in this baselining process of product bundle location in the marketplace and customer needs analysis is the *present and potential customer analysis matrix* shown in Figure 7.3. This analysis is a process utilizing a matrix format to focus a future-focused organization on its

Customers		Expectations of customers	How we meet these expectations	
			Now/ measure	Future/ measure
Current		• Fast service	80%/number shipped on-time	98%/successful field installations
Future		• Ability to customize	50%/ additions customers want	• 100%/response to customer request

Figure 7.3   Present and Potential Customer Analysis Matrix

present and potential customer base. This concept should be used in conjunction with the market field location concept.

Organizations in general tend not to do a very thorough analysis of customer expectations for their product and/or service. This is caused by lack of time, resources, knowledge, and the desire to fully understand their customer's expectations and utilization of their product and/or service.

To complete the matrix, the following steps are required:

1.   Develop a list of current customers. This list should be divided into internal and external customers.

2. For each category (internal or external), sort the customers into logical groupings using an affinity process. For each individual or groupings of internal or external customers, list their present expectations clearly and concisely.

3. For each expectation stated, indicate across from it how the organization now meets it, as well as how it is measured. The measure should ensure that the customer expectation is met. If no measure exists, indicate what should be measured in a different color.

4. Opposite each item identified in step 3, indicate what change, if any, might be made in the future to meet this customer expectation. The measures indicated may be the same as in step 3 or they may be new ones.

5. Repeat steps 1 through 4, but focus on potentially new or future customers. The purpose hierarchy and market field location may be a source of input for these steps.

This baselining process of product bundle location in the marketplace, as well the analysis of the present and future customers, provides a future-focused organization with the data needed to now focus on the process of expanding and redefining their customers' needs.

Many organizations have been successful future-focused organizations in the past as well as currently. Here are some examples of organizations that have successfully changed as their customers' culture and needs changed:

- Filling stations came into existence with the purpose of serving the needs of the motoring public. They initially offered fuel, water, air, and later repair service. As the motoring public's culture changed to one of convenience, they also changed to become minimarts. They are still fulfilling their purpose of service to the motoring public. Today the minimart future-focused organization should be looking and analyzing the trends that may affect motoring travel in the future. How would they respond if today's motoring public shifted to mass transit?

- Pizza shops now have home delivery, which was pioneered by Dominos Pizza. The commercials of a few years ago use to show a person bring home a pizza and the family saying "Cold again!" Home delivery was developed to respond to a need of the customer. Now almost every area in the United States has at least one home delivery service. A future-focused organization would now be thinking of what else can we deliver while we bring the pizza—perhaps an assortment of snacks and drinks on board for the customers to pick from, a portable minimart.

- The town hardware stores have been transformed into home service centers that carry everything needed for the homeowner. Again the customer's culture has been changing over the years to a more do-it-yourself approach. These home centers offer computerized deck design, kitchen and bathroom layout assistance, workshops, videos, self-help books, and so on. They changed in response to the homeowners' changing purposes and needs.

- Insurance agents have changed to become full-service financial planners. They offer insurance and investments now. They are still fulfilling their purpose of helping their customers to provide for the future. They now offer more services to meet their customers needs for preparing for the future. They have expanded their purpose hierarchy to meet a changing customer culture concerning awareness around planning for the future.

- ☞ Catalog companies have expanded from offering ordinary merchandise to catalogs of a specialty nature with high-quality goods to fit a variety of customer needs. We now even have the home shopping network that televises its merchandise. Again these companies are meeting their customer's needs for convenience.

- ☞ Telephone companies have expanded from hard-wired telephone service to more mobile communications. Customers are able to improve their productivity with car and mobile telephones and faxes by eliminating the dead time of commuting and turning it into productive time.

Unfortunately, some major institutions that have not kept pace and changed as their customers' culture moved to new plateaus in their cultural hierarchy. Such are either draining or not developing resources needed by future-focused organization. Capital and knowledge are the two important resources required by the future-focused organization.

These major institutions are government (at all levels) and education (kindergarten to college). These two major institutions have control and influence over the important resources needed by future-focused organization. It is ironic that today these institutions are enthusiastically embracing TQM and at the same time are requesting more tax dollars or additional subsidies. Before either of these two institutions adopts TQM, they should have radical surgery on their infrastructure.

Both institutions need to understand the ever widening gap between their purpose focus and culture and that of their customers. In both institutions a few isolated incidents of a successful short-term use of TQM or some other program of the month can be pointed to as successful intervention. These are isolated incidents and too few to change the entrenched bureaucracy that is in place.

At the governmental level (federal, state, county, and local), they constantly are seeking more tax dollars to foster a bygone era. We do not need to have bigger more costly governments; we need downsized governments that support and foster a business environment. We need governmental units that are cost efficient and not ones that are draining off capital and wasting it. We need governmental units that understand who the customer is and what the customer needs and then respond to these needs with simplified processes.

More tax dollars only support, extend, and solidify the wrong culture. We need to shift governmental bureaucratic thinking from the attitude that the taxpayers exist to support the bureaucracy to the attitude that the bureaucracy exists to support the taxpayer's needs. Once they change their purpose focus and culture and align them with their customers' needs, real change can come about. Once real change is in place, they can then begin TQM and continually improve the right processes.

Our educational institutions are suppose to be the storehouse and inventors of knowledge, which they translate into products that develop trained workers needed for a future-focused organization. Today we read of skyrocketing tuition, high school graduates who do not even have minimal skills after 12 years of education, and professors who teach very little and receive high pay. In addition to these statements the following recent statistics have come forth.

At the College Level

- Teaching assistants and part-time nomad lecturers account for one-third of the nation's collegiate faculty and teach one-half of all undergraduate courses.[1]
- One-third of the faculty at the University of Wisconsin teaches less than one class per year.[2]
- At the City Colleges of Chicago, many faculty member teach less than 15 hours per week.[3]
- Administrative expenses have become the fastest-rising cost on campus.[4]
- An increased emphasis on research has meant that professors spend only 6 hours per week teaching. Yet a college board survey found that half of the professors spent fewer than 5 hours per week in research and a third admit to none at all.[5]

At the High School Level

- Only 29% of employers and 40% of principals say students know enough math to hold entry-level jobs.[6]
- Just 19% of employers and 27% of principals say that students write well enough.[7]

Education's answer to the crises is the same as government—more money. More money to keep up the outdated and outmoded course curriculum and faculty research. A

---

1. R. Grossman and C. Leroux, Radical Idea: Professors in the Classroom, *Chicago Tribune*, Section 4, Sunday, September 13, 1992, p. 1.
2. Ibid.
3. F. James, City Colleges Heading For Faculty Clash, *Chicago Tribune*, Section 2, Sunday, September 13, 1992, p. 1.
4. C. Del Valle, E. Schine, and G. Mc Williams, A Lot Less Moola Moola on Campus, *Business Week*, October 5, 1992, pp. 114–115.
5. Ibid.
6. D. Kelly, High School Grads Lack Job Skills, *USA Today*, Lifeline Section, p. 1D.
7. Ibid.

future-focused organization needs well-trained state-of-the-art graduates and not ones that have to retrained once they are hired.

Many articles today call for the need for educational change and for legislation to accomplish it. They trumpet the fact that public trust is waning. Longer school days and years will not accomplish what is needed. Education needs to focus its processes on its customers and change its culture and processes to deliver what is required. It will mean paying the football coach less than the chancellor and paying the teachers more than both of them. Parents of students need to demand better academic programs rather than better sports programs. The whole educational system and the bureaucrats need radical surgery before they adopt TQM. Continuous improvement of what is in place will not deliver the knowledge worker required by a future-focused organization. A complete reengineering of the educational system from grade 1 through graduate school is required. Higher education has lost sight of its purpose to educate the public[8] and needs to refocus itself.

Summary

Any organization can become a future-focused organization by first understanding its current customers and their needs. Once this is accomplished, a future-focused organization can then begin the process of redefining and reshaping customer expectations. This process is preceded by a complete and exhaustive understanding of the organization's strengths in the marketplace, as well as a detailed understanding of its present and potential customer base.

---

8. A Lot Less Moola Moola on Campus, *Business Week*, October 5, 1992, pp. 11, 115.

The Virtual Super Team

Avoiding the Team-based Silo Syndrome

The idea of high-performance work teams is both old and new. Work teams have been around for years, having grown out of the quality circles movement and other worker-participation programs that have proved successful in Japan and the United States. The *high-performance* aspect is new and gaining more and more interest. Companies are proud to announce that they have "52 teams, up and running for the past 8 years" but they are much more reluctant to tell you what these teams have accomplished in the last 6 months. This is what happens when the number of teams becomes the objective, rather than the "how" to solve pressing organizational problems.

Much has been written about the functional silo organization. Participative teams have provided an excellent alternative to the structured hierarchies of the past. However, teams that are allowed to lie dormant and unproductive accomplish nothing more than to introduce another layer of complexity on the functional silo organization. One executive commented recently, "We used to have functional silos. Now we have a barnyard of programs and a range of teams, and I'm not sure what they're all doing."

The following is a list of reasons for the team-based silo syndrome, sometimes referred to as self-destructive work teams:

- Loss of direction, goals, sponsorship, attention
- Confusion about priorities, conflicting forces, blurred visions
- Ineffective team leadership
- Loss of credibility and integrity
- Absence of team tools (minutes, brainstorm lists, work plans)
- Tenure of team and team members
- Team skill sets versus activities
- Individual team member performance
- Loyalty to the team first, company second
- Closed cultures; no new members allowed
- Other teams are the competition
- Stymied learning; avoiding tough problems
- Localized problem solving
- Spontaneous, irrelevant activities
- Criticism of the teaming process
- Unwillingness to take risks, try new things
- Loss of ownership and commitment
- Activities without real results

Switching from a functional silo organization to a more unstructured teaming process is fairly straightforward, but making it work is far more demanding because people do not become immune to the ongoing problems of the business by forming teams. In many instances, lateral management teams, employee participation, and management by consensus building can take on a life of their own, rather than assisting in actual organizational growth. Does this have to happen? Yes, if a company haphazardly launches a bunch of teams and then expects them to function and evolve on their own. In many cases, companies have provided the means (team-building skills) but not the ends (specific goals and challenges to produce results).

What can be done to make sure organizations do not fall prey to the team-based silo syndrome? The answer is obvious. First, we need to treat lateral management teams as a dynamic process and change their direction and structure whenever it is necessary. Second, we need a simple organizational sensing system that reports regularly or continuously about what is happening with the lateral management teaming process. This system should tell us if the process is in control and provide guidance on how to improve the capability of this process: Are we heading in the right direction? Are we improving our rate of progress? Are our day-to-day actions contributing value to our customers? Are we living the MVP (mission, vision, position)? Companies that allow their teaming process to function without formal measurements and feedback may find themselves disconnected from their vision or making a lot of improvements that are transparent to the customer.

Virtual Super Teams

Virtual super teams (VSTs) are the next generation of lateral management employee involvement teams. They plan and perform work and manage many traditional supervisory, support, or management functions of the past.

VSTs are organized around businesses, product lines, processes, technology, or some hybrid of these. VSTs function as a de facto small business and manage themselves as a self-contained value center (for example, order entry, material planning and control, purchasing, manufacturing, quality, engineering, and customer service). VSTs provide a framework for breaking down a single homogeneous company into non-homogeneous business or value centers.

VSTs possess the basic skills of lateral teaming processes, however, they are advanced in the application of these skills as shown in Figure 8.1. Traditional cross-functional teams are usually involved in improving a procedure, practice, or a small fragment of a business. VSTs are responsible not only for quality, but for every aspect that makes their business within a business successful. They may also evolve into a network of virtual subteams that are focused on reengineering business processes or implementing other changes that support the VSTs success.

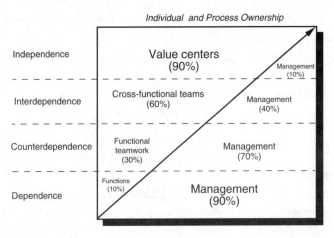

Figure 8.1 Organizational Robustness

Beyond the basic skills of teams, VSTs have developed other skills that have allowed them to advance:

Team Constitution Skills

Team members develop, follow, and enforce the team's own preestablished policies, procedures, goals, and expected performance criteria (rate and magnitude of improvement)—the team's constitution. These rules range from arriving on time to working on issues that are directly linked to the company's MVP. Teams also see a clear relationship between the team's activities and the company's improved competitiveness.

Team Collaboration Skills

Members work together on ideas and solutions or openly seek help outside the team. Facilitation has become internalized by every team member, and every member is conscious about getting 100% of the minds working together. They also provide an environment where members can participate without being ridiculed or ignored.

Team Consensus Skills

Members help each other to reach decisions that make the team successful and that everyone can support and feel ownership toward.

Team Cooperation Skills

Members view conflict and disagreement as a normal activity of the change process. Team members associate change and survival as synonymous, and solutions become clearer when the underlying conflicts become clearer. Members have been developed to handle the emotions of conflict and disagreement and the emotional issues of change.

Team Business Skills

Members are acutely aware of the corporation's challenges and competitive issues, cost and profitability issues, human resource issues, and the like. They have received technical (reengineering, TQM, SPC, JIT, Product Development, DFX) and facilitation (behavioral alignment, team building, conflict, consensus) education so that they can lead the change process. And they receive information openly about the company's and their progress.

Team Boundaryless Skills

Members recognize that success is derived from whatever has to be done to achieve success. They are focused on success and recognize what is needed to achieve success. Teams openly recruit and "plug and play" the skill sets needed to be successful. The distinctions among salary and hourly, departments, functions, management, and employees has gradually become structures that people do not pay much attention to.

VSTs encourage team decision making based on facts, direct experience, and logic that explores and integrates the differences and similarities among team members' points of view. VSTs have also developed a mind-set that "if you're not constantly exploring and implementing change, then you're probably doing only enough to stay even or fall behind the competition."

Very few organizations have successfully implemented VSTs. For those who have, one common observation is the constant tinkering, reshaping, destruction, or creation of new teams. VSTs and their subteams are extremely disciplined, structured, and functional in a snapshot in time. However, they are seamless or virtual in that they can change on a dime and give you nine cents change. They are future-focused.

Organizational Robustness: Integrating VST Activities

Organizational robustness is the transformation to a new organizational model that allows VSTs to function as de facto small businesses. An organization that practices Organizational Robustness faithfully has the following characteristics:

- Boundarylessness, seamlessness
- Flat, fluid, virtual
- One box called the customer success function
- Hierarchy replaced by dynamic, geometric patterns that represent critical customer processes
- Customer need pools, or fractals of resources assembled, reorganized, or redeployed on demand to maximize customer success
- Extremely structured and disciplined, but capable of changing instantaneously and automatically.[1]

Organizational robustness provides the underpinnings for achieving breakthrough results and includes the elements of organizing high-performance teaming structures, developing seamless or process thinking, empowering employees, self-managing the change process, and increasing the rate of team improvements that are linked directly to corporate results. The proper application of these elements is essential for turning around a stagnating continuous improvement effort and achieving real, bottom-line results. Figure 8.2 depicts a conceptual model of what organizational robustness might look like in a snapshot of time where the focus is on a view of the critical processes that deliver the customer the needed products and services. The traditional organization structure

---

1. T. Burton, J. Moran, M. Filipiak, *The Reengineering Toolbox*, The Center for Excellence in Operations, Inc., pp. 58–64.

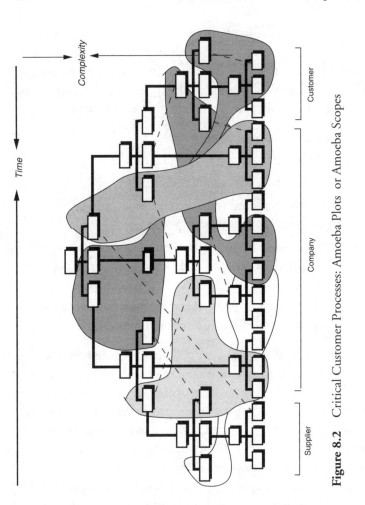

Figure 8.2   Critical Customer Processes: Amoeba Plots or Amoeba Scopes

is in the background and the processes flow throughout it. In a robust organization, the traditional organization chart fades further into the background and the process view comes more to the foreground.

Organizational robustness addresses the softer teaming issues of reengineering and requires a company to internalize the following philosophies and values:

☞ *Awareness, not unconsciousness.* Continuous improvement activities are often based on the assumption that employees have something to learn and that management is the best teacher. Awareness is the value that raises employee consciousness, cognitive powers, and self-fulfillment. It is also the driving force behind breakthrough improvement from multiple directions, not just top down.

☞ *Permissive, not dogmatic.* Management does not know best and employees are smart enough to see the company's problems. Programs that extend this vision of management infallibility stifle employee involvement and creativity. Good programs are permissive when everyone learns from each other, when problems are acknowledged in real time, and when feedback has become a comfortable process.

☞ *Universal, not exclusionary.* Management cannot build success by showing their employees videos about the Japanese or by hiding their critical problems. Successful companies practice complete integrity and honesty in all their dealings with customers, suppliers, and employees. And people need to understand the factors, internal and external, that contribute to corporate (and personal) success. Winning is the objective and shared rewards is the result.

☞ *Education, not training.* Results and breakthrough improvements are not achieved by teaching techniques. In fact, this approach has often been superficial and exploitive to employees. Some organizations are beginning to reference monkeys, dogs and infants when the subject of training is brought up. Employees must be educated to improve their thinking skills (imaging, excellence, innovation, anticipation, divergent and convergent thinking, mapping, visioneering), internalize behavioral change, experience self-renewal, and float up to consciousness. The learning organization and the seamless corporation are merely abstractions until people make them happen.

✎ *Integration, not isolation.* High-performance teaming structures must have clearly defined goals, objectives, milestones and results that are directly linked to the company's mission, vision, and purpose (MVP). Additionally, there must be a central nervous system that integrates and redirects the goals, issues, project activities, and opportunities of the teaming organization. The objective is to create a closed-loop, real time improvement process driven by the MVP.

✎ *Full Participation, not involvement.* Companies use only 10% to 30% of their employees full potential and they have not even begun to unleash these powerful, underemployed resources. Employees can make significant contributions to the quotation, product development, manufacturability, and service areas even though there may not be a formal teaming structure in place. However, employees need to touch, feel, and experience the success of their contributions in an ad hoc improvement situation or their desire to participate will disappear quickly.

✎ *Holistic, not targeted.* People are naturally resentful and distrustful toward business and other forms of institutional leadership because they feel powerless and isolated from their own lives. To the extent that companies can help employees manage a confusing, complex, and sometimes frightening set of circumstances in their own worlds, alienation and distrust can be replaced by confidence, co-destiny, and breakthrough results.

The first aspect of organizational robustness is putting these values into practice, and changing corporate behavior is far easier said than done. Many companies may feel that they have already implemented these values but the reality is that most have not. Taking full advantage of organizational robustness calls for a subtle but profound shift in mind-set: a results-oriented improvement philosophy that develops employees into "outsider/insiders" and that encourages the frequent reengineering of teaming processes to achieve breakthrough results in a short period of time.

A future-focused organization has a defined and ingrained process to help integrate the rich and diverse skills and knowledge base of its employees into powerful functional and/or lateral management planning and problem-solving teams. The lateral management aspect of a future-focused organization is a critical organizational component that must have a clear teaming process in order for company-wide goals to be accomplished efficiently and effectively in a lateral management process.

There are three distinct but integrated aspects of this process to integrate teaming, problem solving, and planning:

- Teaming process
- Communication process
- Planning/problem solving process

The integration of these three distinct aspects is shown in Figure 8.3.

The *virtual super team* (VST) teaming process is the central core of the changeover to a future-focused organization. The integrated model shown in Figure 8.3 has communication

Figure 8.3   Integrative Process

skills as the centerpiece of the model. The problem solving/ planning process highlights the most important elements for the management and associates to work on in order to make change happen. The teaming process and the communication skills drive the activities to accomplish the change elements by focusing on the key interpersonal competencies required for optimal application of any of the quality planning tools.

The remainder of this chapter will present an explanation of each element of the integrated model and then show the results of this integrated process when applied to a management group.

Communication Process

The communication process represents a core set of interpersonal competencies and skills that is essential for an efficient teaming and planning process. The communication process includes the following skills, shown in Figure 8.4:

- Maintain and enhance self-esteem
- Focus on specific behaviors and outcome
- Listen for understanding
- Communicate benefits
- Set goals and follow-up dates
- Reinforce desired behaviors

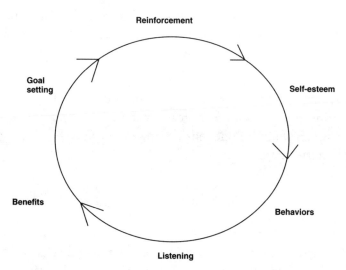

Figure 8.4 Communication Process

The application of these skills to the VST teaming and planning process will lead to improved team performance and higher-quality results from the planning tools.

Maintain and Enhance Self-esteem

Leaders must embrace a style of interacting with employees that will maintain and enhance their self-esteem. Research indicates that there is a clear correlation between group productivity and levels of self-esteem. By fostering an environment of respect for team members, their motivation to perform competently is increased and a richer array of ideas can be generated from the planning tools.

Focus on Specific Behaviors and Outcome

The objective of this skill is to ensure clear communication by avoiding vagueness. When discussing team matters, it is critical that the leader be very specific. Focusing on outcomes ensures that team members will understand how specific behavior will affect others and the goals and objectives of the team.

By focusing on specific behaviors and outcomes, the leader can minimize reactions from team members that refer to attitude or personality, erode self-esteem, and negatively affect the team's performance.

Listen for Understanding

Effective leaders are excellent listeners. Listening is an active process that includes *hearing* what a team member is saying and responding in a way that lets others know that they are being heard. Paraphrasing is an effective way of summarizing what someone has said. In a team setting it can serve to clarify for both the person speaking and other group members. The management and planning tools are most effective when a variety of perspectives is presented. The successful team leader maintains an environment that promotes clear communication within the team.

Communicate Benefits

Teams are more likely to be productive when members clearly understand how the goals of the team are of benefit to the company, the department, or the team members themselves. In the process of communicating benefits, leaders provide a motivational framework for team members. Benefit statements should identify the needs of the individuals and/or the organization and articulate how the team relates to those needs.

Set Goals and Follow-up Dates

Goal setting provides a framework for communication with team members. Teams are more productive when leaders effectively communicate goals and assess the team's progress toward those goals. Goals provide objective criteria to use in reviewing the team's performance. Team goals are most effective when they are presented in the context of the larger business perspectives of the organization. Follow-up dates increase the likelihood that goals will be accomplished by increasing the probability of follow-up.

Reinforce Desired Behaviors

In virtually all VST teaming situations, a knowledge of how to use reinforcement techniques to shape behavior is necessary if a leader is to have some control over the productivity of the team. A leader is constantly challenged to increase team productivity.

To encourage productive behaviors, the leader rewards individual team members or the entire team after they have demonstrated appropriate behaviors. Rewards can come in the form of introducing something desirable, such as recognition or praise.

Virtual Super Team Teaming Process

The VST teaming process is an important dimension of the reengineering and advanced total quality movement. Organizations have discovered the benefits of involving employees at all levels in teams. Interaction with other employees is a good source of learning and stimulation. Using the management and planning tools in a team setting enhances the effectiveness of the tools and capitalizes on the creativity and energy generated by the dynamics of the team.

Productive, high-performance VSTs share the following characteristics:

- The goals of the team are communicated to and understood by all members of the team.

- Team members are clear on their roles in the team.

- The resources the team will need have been identified and secured.

- Information exchange systems have been developed to promote communication among team members.

- Decision-making tools are used at appropriate junctures in the life of the team.

- Over time the distinctions among facilitator, leader, and team member disappear as these activities are integrated into the VST process.

In addition, the team leader should match her or his style to the task of the group. For example, when using a planning tool, team members might need direction and instruction. The leader must provide members with this information and take a directive posture. Once this direction is clear, the task might require group participation. At this point, the leader needs to help the group process the information. At this point, it would be more appropriate for the team leader to be facultative. If the leader does not match his or her behavior to the task of the group, communication will break down, creativity will be stifled, and the management and planning tools will lose their effectiveness. Figure 8.5 shows the details of the teaming process.

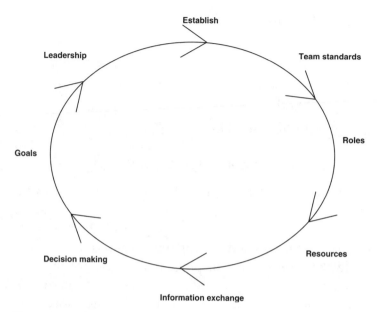

Figure 8.5 Teaming Process

Establish Virtual Super Teams

In organizations, strategic planning goals are often accomplished through efforts of project teams and dynamically interactive work groups.

More and more basic inventions, minor and major breakthroughs, and creative inspirations stem from group collaboration. When individuals work in a truly collaborative way, the product development cycle is abbreviated, innovation flourishes, and there is a more timely response to the marketplace.

Achievement of fully functional VSTs means that the leader must concentrate on eight important areas:

1. Establish the team.
2. Set high performance team standards.

3. Clarify roles.
4. Identify and secure resources.
5. Implement an information exchange mechanism.
6. Apply management and decision-making tools.
7. Establish goals.
8. Institute leadership.

Virtual Super Team Standards

Every VST that is established needs to set and measure a set of team standards or codes of conduct. VSTs need to set guidelines as to how they will function. Everyone on the team needs to be part of the standards-setting process and actively participate in the measurement of progress in implementing these agreed upon standards. As a rule of thumb, no more than 10 standards should be set and measured on a regular basis. Some team standards could be set by management and be common to all teams. The measurement of the standards is important, since the team members will see the positive results by adhering to the team standards as well as the negative consequences of not meeting the standards. Some VST standards that could be considered are the following:

- Shared leadership
- Mutual respect
- Commitment
- Energy and enthusiasm
- Resolving conflict
- Respect
- Valuing others opinion
- Accountability
- Attendance

- Focused meetings
- Closure on issues
- Effective use of time

The team standards should be measured on a regular basis by the team. At the end of a team meeting, a rating form such as the one shown in Figure 8.6 should be filled in by each team member and evaluated by the leader and the results shared with the team. As the team matures, the measurement can be done in real time by polling the team and making it an interactive exercise. Usually, in the early team formation stages it may be necessary to use a secret ballot technique to draw in everyone's input. The scoring system is as follows:

1, poor performance and needs immediate attention

3, marginal performance; group is working but not functioning efficiently

5, good performance, keep monitoring

7, world class performance

Roles

The players on a team need to understand very clearly their precise roles. In each team there needs to be a team sponsor, team leader, team facilitator, and team members. Since so much has been written on these particular roles, it will not be repeated here. Specific guidelines need to be established for each role so that confusion and overlap of responsibilities can be avoided.

Resources

Teams will need resources that they can draw on as they go through either the planning or problem-solving process that has been assigned. These resources should have been anticipated by the team sponsor in advance and provision made to

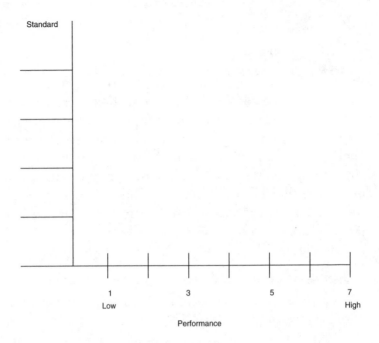

Figure 8.6   Team Standards Measurement

provide them when requested. A team sponsor can utilize the SMART matrix shown in Figure 8.12 to help plan for resources. Failure to provide adequate resources to a sponsored team can cause frustration on the part of team members, since they will not be able to complete their assigned responsibilities in a timely manner. Adequate resources are one ingredient to ensure success.

Information Exchange

Teams need a way to share information on a regular and timely manner. Team meetings do not necessarily guarantee information exchange unless active listening is practiced by the team members. The team leader must work to ensure that information is made available to all team members using all means available. It is better to overcommunicate than to undercommunicate.

Decision Making

The decision-making process for a team engaged in planning or problem solving needs to be structured and disciplined. The structure and discipline fit into the team standards section as a needed element. A teaming process model is shown in Figure 8.5.

Goals

Every team needs to have definitive goals that detail what is expected of it and in what time frame. These goals should be included in the initial team charter that the sponsor develops. The goals can be refined during periodic reviews. Without clear goals, teams can make many false starts and spend a large amount of time trying to define what they are suppose to be doing.

Leadership

Effective leaders are effective communicators. Effective means that they first listen to make sure that they hear what others are saying and then respond in a way that shows others that they have been heard and understood. This helps to make them skillful at establishing rapport with other people and able to be problem solvers even in confused or emotionally charged situations. Leaders need to be skillful at the following:

- Acknowledging what individuals say
- Paraphrasing what individuals say
- Actively listening to individuals

Every leader knows that to be effective he or she needs to communicate clearly. One way to do this when discussing job-related matters is by being specific about what someone is doing or saying. This puts the focus on the employee's behavior or action, rather than on his or her attitude or personality. Focusing on outcomes refers to how the specific behavior affects others or the environment. Focusing on the outcomes of a specific behavior helps the employee to see the importance in addressing that behavior.

The leader is faced daily with the challenges of helping his or her people to become more effective and productive. This involves influencing employees to use more of those behaviors that improve performance and fewer of those behaviors that cause it to deteriorate.

One way to get more of what you want from employees, and less of what you do not want, involves the skillful use of reinforcement techniques. Over time, these will bring about a gradual change in an employee's performance. The three techniques are as follows:

1. Introduce rewards.
2. Introduce negative consequences.
3. Ignore.

Strengthening the employee's perception of self-competency is synonymous with effective leadership. Maintaining and enhancing self-esteem is a critical leadership skill because of the great impact self-esteem has on job performance.

Research has demonstrated that employees are motivated to work at a level consistent with their perception of self-competency. If an individual feels competent in performing a task, he or she will perform or be highly motivated to perform in a manner consistent with those feelings. Similarly, if an employee perceives himself or herself as less than competent in a particular dimension of the job, his or her performance in that area will be negatively affected.

Planning Process

The planning process, as shown in Figure 8.7 provides a systematic and disciplined approached to planning. The output of one step is the input to the next step. This process utilizes tools and techniques that help a team see the issue that they are working on in a holistic sense, and they focus in on the key elements to investigate further.

Understanding the Problem's Magnitude

Organizations need an assessment process that graphically depicts its strengths, weaknesses, and opportunities for improvement. An organizations needs a clear and concise baseline picture of where it is starting from before it begins any transformation journey.

A base-lining process presents an opportunity for a future-focused organization to develop a management consensual

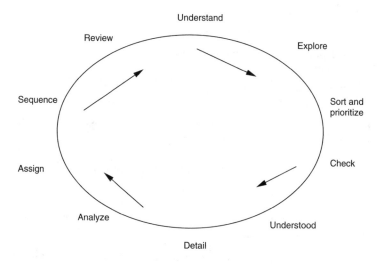

Figure 8.7   Planning Process

picture of itself. A base-lining process is a top-management-driven process of frank and honest assessment of a set of measurement criteria done at all levels. The measurement criteria should include most of the following elements:

- Organizational culture
- Daily work environment
- Leadership: top, middle, and supervisory
- Customer–supplier partnerships
- Communication effectiveness
- Decision making with fact
- Training
- Customer commitment
- Planning process
- Team constitution skills
- Team collaboration skills
- Team consensus skills
- Team cooperation skills
- Other organizational specific areas

A *radar chart*, as shown in Figure 8.8, is a tool that can be used to record the assessments. Each spoke on the radar chart represents one of the measurement criteria chosen. Many different scales can be used, as follows:

- Qualitative: strongly disagree to strongly agree
- Quantitative: 1 (low) to 5 (high)

The scale of measurement is set up so that the farther from the center, the better the score.

Base-lining assessments take at least a 4-hour session with a top executive group to complete. Usually, this is the first time

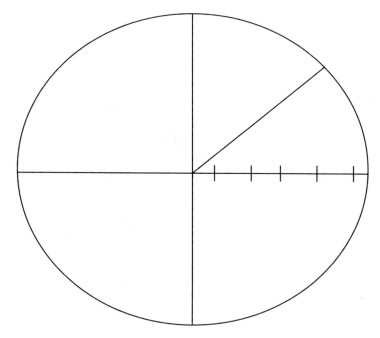

Figure 8.8   Radar Chart

the group has met as a team to openly discuss their views on the organization's position. During this session they will begin to develop a holistic organizational view. After each criterion is scored, the team leader or facilitator can connect the dots representing the consensus on each. The resulting shape shows where the organization is now, as shown in Figure 8.9.

The next step in the process is to do a sanity check with others in the organization, as well as customers, and make any modifications based on their feedback or insight. In addition, members of the assessment group can do this same exercise with members of their staff in order to get an assessment picture of how their organizational units see the strengths, weaknesses, and opportunities of the current system.

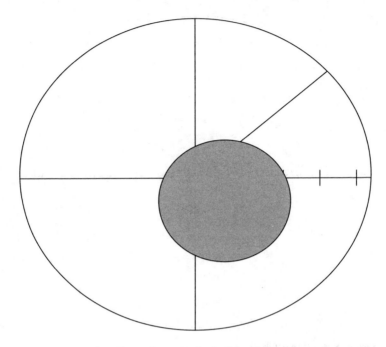

Figure 8.9   Radar Chart: Organization's Current Position

The visual image developed using a base-lining instrument is not a static visualization. The image will change as the organization transforms itself, as consumer demands change, and as employees become empowered. It is important to continually monitor the change on a periodic basis by developing new measurement criteria that depict the future demands being placed on the organization.

Explore

In this step we explore the issues that are involved in improving a particular criterion identified in the previous step. One process that is helpful in exploring an issue is the affinity diagram process.

The card sort or affinity process[2] takes large amounts of data, ideas, concepts, and suppositions and provides a structured process to sort them into similar patterns or relationships. The output of this process can be utilized in numerous ways and provides the basis for using other thinking tools on the sorted output. This process provides the best results with groups of between four and eight individuals.

The information to be sorted can be generated in a variety of ways. Often the information is generated from a brainstorming session with the team members. This type of session usually generates at least 100 ideas, which are then arranged into similar groupings and each grouping is given a descriptive header card.

Sort and Prioritize

A prioritization process is needed to narrow down the major issues that surfaced during the affinity process to a few key issues. We must prioritize since we usually do not have all the resources necessary or available to do everything at the same time. There are a number of prioritization processes,[3] which range from voting techniques to a more rigorous pairwise comparison process.

The pairwise comparison process is an efficient method to reach group consensus on the most important issues. In the pairwise comparison method, each issue generated in the affinity process is assigned a weight based on its contribution to accomplishing the stated purpose. Each issue statement is

---

2. G. Hoffherr, *The Toolbook, Decision Making and Planning for Optimum Results*, Markon, Inc., 1993, pp. 15–16.
3. Ibid., pp. 7, 17, 25, and 27.

compared to all the other statements in a two at a time fashion using the following scale:

1: The components are of equal importance in accomplishing the purpose.

5: One component is significantly more important than another component in accomplishing the purpose.

10: One component is exceedingly more important than another component in accomplishing the purpose.

1/5: One component is significantly less important than another component in accomplishing the purpose.

1/10: One component is exceedingly less important than another component in accomplishing the purpose.

A total score is computed for each issue category and then rank ordered so that the team members could then decide on the most important issues to pursue. The higher the score achieved, the more important is the issue.

This process develops a team consensus to follow around the path and instills a sense of ownership in the chosen paths. This ownership creates the will or spirit in the team to follow through. Figure 8.10 shows a prioritization matrix.

Check

After the sorting process has been accomplished and the key issues have been identified, we need to examine how well we are doing currently on each. The importance of the issue can now be compared to its performance. The best issues to pursue are those that are important as well as in need of improvement. A radar chart, describe earlier, is an excellent tool to use to show how issues are developing.

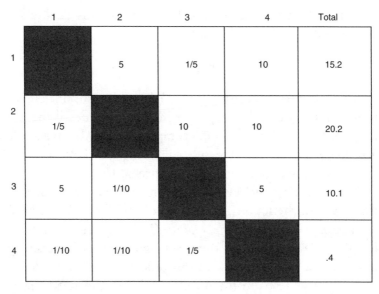

	1	2	3	4	Total
1		5	1/5	10	15.2
2	1/5		10	10	20.2
3	5	1/10		5	10.1
4	1/10	1/10	1/5		.4

Figure 8.10   Prioritization Matrix

Understood

In this step of the planning the team reviews the original statement of the issue and decides, after doing the previous four steps in the model, if there is still agreement that the original issue statement was correct. Usually, at this point it is quite common for the team members to make modifications to the original issue statement. The previous four steps have allowed the team members to view the original issue statement in a holistic manner and have pulled them out of their functional perspective by inputting and synthesizing new information from the other team members. The tools used in the previous four steps, affinity process and the prioritization matrix, force the team members to actively listen to other viewpoints as they affect the original issue statement. Now the issue is really understood, and there is consensus on the key elements that make up this issue.

Details

A tree diagram[4] approach is utilized in this step, since it is a tool that systematically maps out in increasing detail the full range of tasks that need to be accomplished in order to achieve a primary goal and related subgoals. This tool helps to keep the team focused on only the details related to the goal.

As we develop the levels of the tree diagram from left to right, we ask the following question of each level: *What needs to happen for this to be accomplished?* This question helps to focus the development of the tree diagram in an increasingly more logical level of detail. In this process there is a tendency to make large leaps in the detailing process and not to have logical connecting flows. A second questioning process that proceeds from right to left (from the details to the solution option's primary level) through the tree diagram helps to identify these large leaps. The question we ask from right to left is *If these items happen will the next level occur?* If we have made large leaps in detail, we are able to see the disconnect very quickly. Figure 8.11 shows the tree diagram structure.

Analyze and Assign

Assigning and analyzing the key tasks that have been prioritized is a step in the quality planning process. It was designed to focus the planning team on what is involved to accomplish the key tasks.

For each of the key tasks, the planning team needs to determine who will be assigned to the task, what resources will be

---

4. Ibid., pp. 31–32.

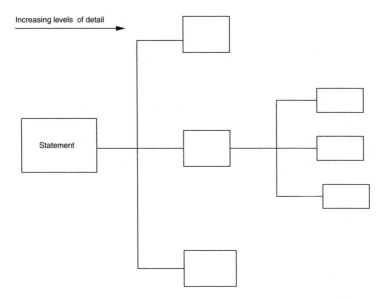

Figure 8.11   Tree Diagram

required, how much time will be involved, and how success will be measured. This step helps the planning team to clarify its description of the scope of the task that they are assigning. In addition, they can uncover any unrealistic assumptions and lofty goals that are not achievable.

As part of this analysis, the planning team should also identify potential obstacles that could affect the successful completion of the task. They should identify both positive and negative forces affecting the task.

A *force field analysis*[5] is a tool that can accomplish this part of the assign and analyze step. The force field analysis encourages team members to raise questions and concerns throughout the process. These concerns and questions are not to be considered as obstacles to successful planning, but should

5. Ibid., p. 35.

instead be valued and not crushed. A SMART matrix,[6] as shown in Figure 8.12, can be used in this step. An explanation of the SMART matrix is given in Chapter 5.

Specifics	Measures	Accountable	Resources	Time

Figure 8.12 SMART Matrix

---

6. Ibid., p. 33.

Sequence and Track

One major task for the planning team is to sequence the various tasks that they have assigned. Tools to sequence tasks range from sophisticated to simple depending on the detail necessary to track a project.

The most visual tool and the easiest to maintain is the Gantt chart,[7] since it can show both work planned and work accomplished on the same chart. This chart visually shows the planning team where projects are ahead of schedule and which projects are behind and need attention, as well as a general sequencing of activities.

The Gantt chart is a simple but very powerful visual tool for sequencing and tracking tasks.

Review

The planning team should hold regular review sessions with those individuals and teams assigned activities and tasks to be accomplished. These review sessions are an integral part of the sequence and track step of the planning process. They should focus on the gaps from the planned completion dates, both positive and negative, indicated on the Gantt chart. Focusing on the gaps forces the planning team to identify factors contributing to the success as well as the failure of the project. This understanding can then be transmitted to other teams to help them to either build on their successes or to avoid their mistakes.

---

7. Ibid., pp. 41–42.

Summary

Communication skills, teams, and the management decision and planning tools are each important elements of a future-focused organization. By combining these elements, maximum efficiency can be gained and the results of the planning process will be optimized.

Figure 8.13 details the overall integrated teaming and planning model, which utilizes a planning process in conjunction with teaming and communication skills to produce an integrated process.

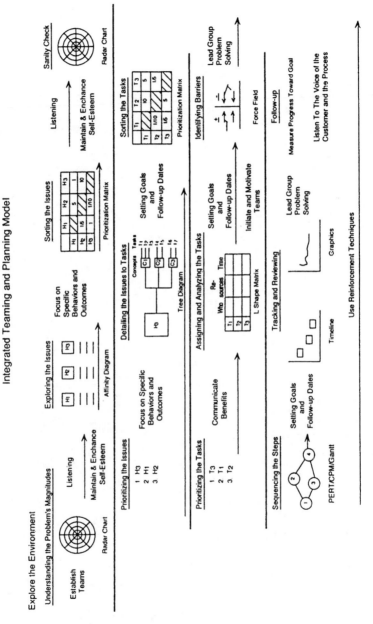

Figure 8.13   Integrated Teaming and Planning Model

The Hiring, Growing, and Rewarding Process[1]

In a future-focused organization, hiring, growing, and rewarding personnel are critical processes for long-term survival.[2] This process of hiring, growing, and rewarding personnel should be approached as a strategic opportunity for your organization. Unfortunately, it is not taken seriously in most organizations today. Too often, today, positions are filled to keep work flowing, rather than ensuring that a long-term flexible productive employee is hired. Future-focused organizations constantly need to rethink and reengineer their current hiring, evaluation, pay, and promotion processes. These critical processes must keep pace with a changing economy and a changing work force's needs and expectations.

The authors wish to thank Joann DeMott, The J. DeMott Co., Philomath, Oregon, and John Hoffman, president of John Hoffman and Associates, New York, for their assistance in the preparation of this chapter.

1. J. DeMott, J. Hoffman, and J. Moran, Hiring and Growing Personnel in a Quality Environment, Abstracts of the *6th Annual Quality Management Conference,* January 26, 1994.
2. C. Collett, J. DeMott, and J. Moran, *Introduction to Critical Processes,* GOAL/QPC Application Report, No. 92-01A, GOAL/QPC, Methuen, Mass., 1992.

What is it we are hiring? A set of skills? The potential to do the job with some training? The spirit of the individual to assimilate into our culture and embrace change? We are hiring all three, but today organizations usually only look at the mental skill set and show little concern about the spirit.

There is an old saying that the mind is willing but the spirit is weak. We need to ensure in our interview, evaluation, pay, and promotion processes that we look both at the mental skill set as well as the willingness of the spirit. The person may have the mental capacity to do the job, but the spirit is needed to move and embrace the mission of the organization. A willing spirit is needed to accept change as an ongoing process.

In a future-focused organization, interviewing looks for a mental and spirit skill set that supports the organization's purpose and cultural philosophy in every worker hired and promoted. These skill sets apply to all positions in the organization and are a basis for all job positions. Over time the philosophy of the organization becomes an invisible and interwoven thread holding the organization together because of such workers.

We must remember that it is the people in the organization who create, apply, and store the organization's knowledge. Without the full cooperation of their minds and spirits there is no effective organization. When the mind and skill sets of all employees are in balance and focused on achieving the organization's purpose, the organization has a soul that allows it to create things in the marketplace and in the workplace.

If we treat hiring as a noncritical process and view it only as keeping work flowing, we should not be surprised when we find that a significant percentage of our employees do not fit in. The result of this poor fit is that the organization has difficulty moving forward toward its vision since significant resistance is encountered.

Hiring and Growing Personnel

Today, in our interviewing, we should be looking for a mental and spirit skill set that supports a future-focused organization philosophy in every worker we hire and promote. Too often we only look for these skill sets in individuals who will directly support a particular effort: the quality manager, the quality coordinator, the facilitator, the materials manager, the manufacturing supervisor, and so on. These skill sets should apply to all positions in the future-focused organization and should be a basis for all job positions.

Table 9.1 provides a list of potential future-focused organization skill and spirit attributes that should be interviewed for in a candidate search. Depending on the job title and purpose, some attributes are definite musts and will not be compromised on. Some attributes are wants or desires and could be developed if we find a suitable candidate who is not totally qualified. There should be a mixture of skills and spirit in choosing the must and want attributes to ensure that we find a capable and willing worker.

Figure 9.1 shows a proposed *position selection summary form* that could be used as a summary document of all interviewed candidates.

Evaluation of Personnel

From the authors' experience and research, the following evaluation axioms have been developed:

Table 9.1   Skill and Spirit Attributes

Attributes	Skill	Spirit
1. Customer orientation		×
2. Makes decisions with data	×	
3. Influences without authority	×	
4. Empowers others	×	
5. Analytical ability	×	
6. Conceptual ability	×	
7. Participative style		×
8. Supports team recognition		×
9. Willingness to accept change		×
10. Uses cost/benefit analysis	×	
11. Persistent		×
12. Coalition building ability	×	
13. Uses the quality process	×	
14. Looks for hidden interrelationships	×	
15. Ability to identify obstacles		×
16. Conveys the quality message		×
17. Insists on measurement	×	
18. Focus on resource optimization	×	
19. Communicates clearly and often	×	
20. Active listener	×	
21. Honest	×	
22. Reliable		×
23. Flexible	×	
24. Nonjudgmental		×
25. Respect for individuality		×

- Workers want to know how they are doing on a regular basis, but do not want to be rated or compared to others.

- Workers want to improve, yet they rarely have the ongoing data and improvement process to do so.

- Workers do not trust or value supervisory evaluations since they are biased; it is how the supervisor feels about the worker.

- Workers desire a position description that clearly delineates the following:

  ✗ What is the purpose of the job?

  ✗ What is the title of the job?

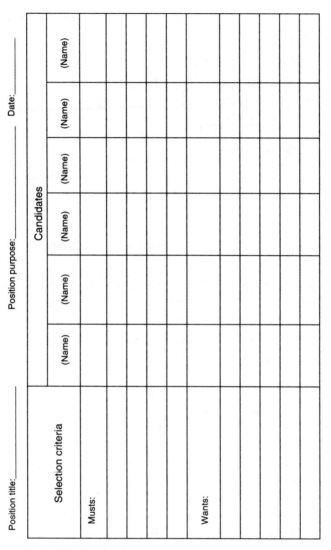

Figure 9.1   Position Selection Summary Form

✗   What department is it in?
✗   Who are the cooperators for this position?
✗   Who do I interact with?

✗ Who are the internal and external customers for this position?

✗ What are the measures of success?

✗ How will I know if I am doing a good job?

✗ From where or whom do I get the information to monitor my measures?

✗ What is my reward?

This is summarized in the *position description form* shown Figure 9.2.

✏ Current evaluation systems either give the worker a treat (money) or a trick (no money). Either can have a detrimental impact on motivation and productivity. Neither experience leaves a worker with a positive memory. The compensation process becomes one that is distrusted and feared. The point is that performance appraisals are, at best, subjective. At worst, performance appraisals are weapons that can be used by managers and supervisors to devastate an employee.

A Proposal for a New System

A new system of evaluation, personal growth, and monetary reward must be developed. This new system must have the following attributes:

✏ Each position has a known purpose that supports the organization's mission and goals.

✏ Each task and activity performed in the position must support the purpose.

✏ The position's purpose is focused on its internal and external customers.

Title of position: _____ Department: _____

Purpose of position: _____ Pay position: _____

Critical processes: Name of process:	Cooperators	Customers	Measures

Figure 9.2 Position Desciption Form

● The worker collects and displays current performance data on all aspects of his or her position and can determine where improvement is needed.

● Workers are empowered to make needed improvements and do so.

- ☞ Workers are trained and proficient in the use of quality problem-solving tools.

- ☞ A worker's performance is reviewed from many views or perspectives such as their cooperatives, customers, and coach.

- ☞ Pay scale increases can occur when increased competencies are achieved, mastered, demonstrated, and shared with cooperatives. These pay scale changes are not tied to performance ratings. This will minimize the competition for raises and topping out by long-term employees.

    This process will help to develop a supportive educational environment among cooperatives that will be conducive to continued improvement and cooperation. This reward system will be immediate rather than one that rewards past accomplishments. Rewards that relate to current accomplishments give the worker the desire to excel even further in the future. They help to set higher-level goals.

A *personal growth form* is shown in Figure 9.3.

Training now becomes an integral part of the growth of a worker. Training now stops being an event that interrupts the normal work routine. It becomes an ongoing pathway for growth.

Workers will be allowed to control their individual changes since they can pick the pace at which they master and demonstrate new job competencies. Change now is viewed as something that they can control and that will provide new opportunities. Change is now a positive rather than a negative force.

Workers will also see customer focus and quality as a vehicle for continuous improvement and personal growth. Customer focus and quality will not have a strong negative aspect that is

Job-related competencies	Achieved	Mastered	Demonstrated	Shared	Pay value	
					Required	Valued added

Figure 9.3 Personal Growth Form

only discussed when something goes wrong, but are now part of the day-to-day work fabric. Customer focus and quality become integrating forces for continuous and lasting improvement.

Workers will view supervisors as mentors, facilitators, and coaches who help guide individuals and teams toward continuous growth and improvement.

A *position improvement form* should be filled out as shown in Figure 9.4 to help facilitate the process described. This form should become a permanent part of each worker's employment history.

Reward and Compensation Systems

Does a perfect compensation system exist? If this system exists, does it treat everyone fairly? Does everyone affected by the compensation system view it as fair? Traditional compensation systems that were designed for a functional organizational environment are running into trouble as the functional organization structure comes under pressure to dissolve or restructure. As cross-functional organizational systems come more to the forefront, rigid functional compensation systems will have to be replaced.

In a future-focused organization the reward and compensation system moves away from the one-dimensional functional view to a multidimensional view. New behaviors are constantly introduced in a future-focused organization, which requires the addition of more multidimensional reward methods, while older outdated methods are dropped, as shown in Figure 9.5. This adding and deleting of components of the reward and recognition system is complimentary to adding, preserving, and deleting attributes of culture in the cultural hierarchy (see Figure 1.1). The changing reward system becomes the "how" to make cultural change a reality.

Many methods of compensation will contribute to the employees total compensation. Some of that compensation will be flexible or variable and some will be fixed as a base pay.

Title of position _____   Department _____

Purpose of position _____   Date _____

Critical process	Improvement opportunity goal	Team/individual	Results achieved (months)					Reasons goal not achieved
			3	6	9	12	15	

Figure 9.4 Position Improvement Form

Employee performance

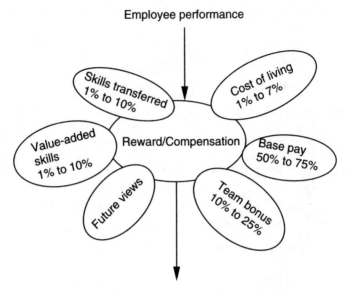

Best overall system effort

Figure 9.5 Compensation Views

In future-focused organization, compensation will be made up of many variable parts, adding up to as much as 40% of an employee's reward or compensation. Variable compensation at all levels will be a common part of future-focused organization compensation systems, which reward bottom-line results and not activities, as today's systems do.

The compensation and hiring systems in a future-focused organization are two critical processes that directly relate to the bottom line. A future-focused organization constantly faces the challenge of balancing employee rewards with performance, as shown in Figure 9.6.

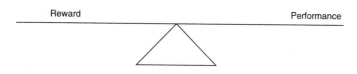

Figure 9.6   The Delicate Balance

Summary

The criteria utilized for the selection of employees and the process established for their development will have a tremendous impact on the long term growth, profitability, and survival of today's corporations. The thoughtful application of selection criteria to the hiring process ensures that newly hired employees have the necessary skills and spirit to flourish as individuals and to make valuable business contributions to the corporation, schools, and agencies. Shared responsibility for employee development makes performance management a two-way process of communication of needs and goals and leads to the continuous improvement of organizational processes and individual achievement.

By defining corporate values and making them an explicit part of the selection and development of individuals, organizations will make tremendous strides toward enhancing and retaining the human capital of the organization.

Charting and
Staying the Course

Charting the course of a future-focused organization is one outcome of the planning process developed in Chapter 5. Staying the course is the deployment part of the planning process. Staying the course is similar to Dr. Deming's point number 1, "create constancy of purpose" and point number 2, "adopt the new philosophy."[1]

1. *Constancy of Purpose:* Create a constancy of purpose for improvement of product and service. A major differentiation between a future-focused organization and other organizations is that the future-focused organization is planning to be the market leader, the most competitive, most profitable and cost-effective producer with a never ending commitment to quality. Its future focus helps it to plan for and be prepared for the problems of tomorrow.

---

1. Mary Walton, *Deming Management at Work,* G.P. Putnam's Sons, New York, 1990, p. 17.

A future-focused organization knows its marketplace and is continually identifying gaps that must be acted on to keep it the market leader. The purpose plot and purpose gap matrix tools introduced in this chapter can be utilized to accomplish this task.

2. *Adopt the new philosophy:* A future-focused organization understands its marketplace and the ongoing economic changes that are taking place. It understands that the marketplace and its customers expect better workmanship each year. Complacency with today's accepted defect levels will cause organizations to lose market share and customers quickly. A future-focused organization defines quality as it applies to its particular circumstances and marketplace. This definition is understood and continually put into practice at all levels in the organization.

Adopting the new philosophy requires a future-focused organization to deal with the uncertainty and obstacles that will arise by producing the necessary resources and support systems. Fear of change in a future-focused organization must be constantly addressed because it is a type of organization that is in constant change. The employees must embrace and not fear change.

A future-focused organization has, as a key part of its new philosophy, a strong focus on productivity. This productivity focus is not only stressed internally but also externally with its suppliers. Suppliers must be treated as part of the family and be partners with the future-focused organization. The future-focused organization must nurture suppliers about accepting change the same way that they do for their own employees. This helps improve quality and the work environment.

Suppliers to a future-focused organization must be taught about their responsibilities for quality. Suppliers are in partnership with a future-focused organization to deliver the value-added product or service to the customer requesting it. Suppliers should become members of some future-focused organization lateral teams, making it possible for everyone involved in the product or service delivery to work for the good of the organization. Suppliers to a future-focused organization are viewed as a part of the organization's soul, as discussed in Chapter 4.

In a future-focused organization, constancy of purpose is defined to be a blend of the understood purpose, the uniqueness or differentiation of the organization in the marketplace, and the organization's core competencies, as shown in Figure 10.1. The constancy of purpose in a future-focused organization gives the organization a sense of stability in difficult times. The course is plotted and being followed continuously. The constancy of purpose in a future-focused organization allows for *"what"* and *"how"* plans are to be formulated that

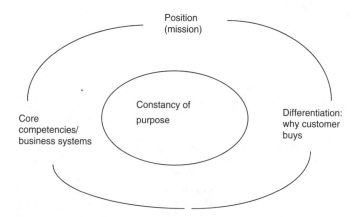

Figure 10.1   Constancy of Purpose

sum up to a budget and focused people activities, as shown in Figure 10.2. The *"what"* plans delineate the product and services that we will offer to the marketplace. The *"how"* plans detail how we will accomplish the delivery.

Staying the course involves the alignment of key critical systems and critical cultural philosophies. This alignment helps to produce the desired behaviors in the organization needed to produce the business outcomes to achieve the plan.

In many organizations that we have consulted with the lament from senior executives is always: "We do a great job planning. We plan for everything and unfortunately we never execute any of the plans."

Execution or staying the course is a very difficult task since we can encounter all the potential obstacles to failure. It may seem at times to be an overwhelming task. Two tools will now be discussed that can aid a future-focused organization in staying the course: the *purpose plot* and the *purpose gap matrix*.

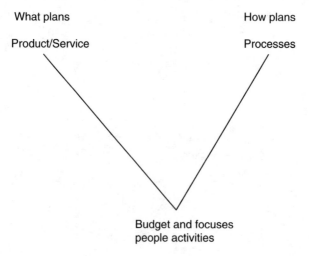

Figure 10.2   Plans to Budget

With the purpose plot tool, future-focused organizations can chart the past history of their organizations, as well as make predictions for the future.

The *purpose plot* is a way for an organization to track and project how past, current, and potential organizational milestones have affected or will affect the organization, either positively or negatively. The purpose plot is a tool that has been designed to both track past history but help predict the future impact of decisions being made today.

Organizational milestones can be a product or service introduction, a corporate reorganization, a change of leadership, mergers, takeovers, technological breakthroughs, and so on. Figure 10.3 shows the purpose plot tool. On the horizontal axis in the middle of the purpose plot we begin a time plot from the start of the organization to 5 years into the future. For each year plotted we identify key milestones, both positive and negative, that have had a major influence on the organization.

The senior executive team doing the plot then assesses each milestone for its impact as either low, medium, or high in a positive or negative direction. The milestone is then plotted and identified on the graph. The effect of each milestone that is past history is easy to plot since its impact is known with certainty. Current and future milestones, once estimated as to their potential impact, must be monitored. A milestone initially identified as positive may later turn out to have a negative impact. Conversely, some initially identified negative milestones could turn out positive. Thus it is important to continually monitor and periodically assess the impact of these milestones.

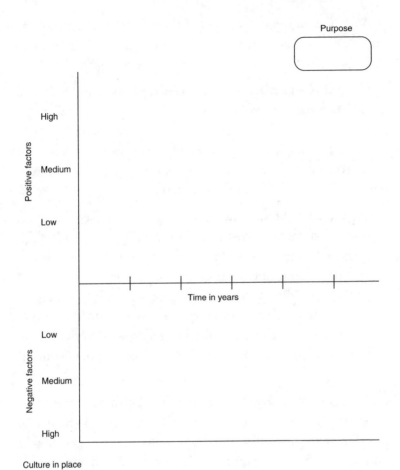

Figure 10.3   Purpose Plot

Examples of milestones that can shift in their initial estimated impact are the following:

- A new product is announced but it is 16 months late getting to the market.
- A new product has to be recalled or retrofitted.

☍   A new supercomputer chip is announced, but the products that it will be used in will not be available for another year. Sales of existing products decrease rapidly.

☍   A new product or service is announced, but the competition beats you to the market and has a lower price.

The purpose plot should be used in conjunction with the purpose and cultural hierarchies as shown in Chapter 4.

The other tool that can help a future-focused organization to stay the course is the *purpose gap matrix*. This tool is a summary matrix that records and displays the action plans developed by the senior executive team to help them close documented gaps that exist between the current performance or position of the organization and the purpose it should be achieving. The purpose gap matrix is shown in Figure 10.4.

In the first column, each gap documented is stated as specifically as possible and the amount of the gap is stated quantitatively (numeric or percentage). The second column states any specific short-term action plans that may be undertaken to attempt to close the gap it is directed toward. The amount of the gap anticipated to be closed is also stated. The short-term action plans are usually reactive in nature since they have a short time horizon to close a limited amount of the gap documented.

The last column contains the long-term action plans to close the documented gap and to get the organization back to its purpose level of performance. Each action plan is specific, with the amount and timing of the gap closure clearly indicated.

This matrix can be used by the senior executive planning team to track and monitor progress toward purpose gap closure.

PURPOSE

Specify/quantify gaps to be closed	Action plans	
	1 year*	3 years

* Short-term action plans to close gaps consistent with plans identified to close 3-year gaps

Figure 10.4 Purpose Gap Matrix

Behavioral Alignment

The future-focused organization is an aligned organization. However, the quality of this alignment is only as good as the collective individuals that make up the organization. Therefore, a critical element of organizational alignment is behavioral alignment.

Most organizations jump on the "river" of continuous improvement, TQM, Reengineering, TPM, and EDI programs without ever recognizing the linkages between where the company really needs to be and the results needed from these activities to support success. In a short period of time, resources get caught up in their own currents:

- Current fears

- Current issues (of the minute)

- Current politics

People merely "go with the flow." They become part of the invisible mass of people who are directed by the environment instead of by their own values. People need to realize when they have become part of the problem rather than part of the solution.

Our beliefs and our personal system of how we process beliefs have the power to create or destroy a reengineering (or any other improvement) effort. Every experience in an individual's life is a perception or a generalization subject to interpretation. Individual behavior is a direct result of how people perceive these experiences. Once accepted, our beliefs become unquestioned commands to our nervous system. The patterns of people's belief systems can cause them to feel helpless about change. They have the power to expand or limit the possibilities of our present and future (company, professional, personal, social, educational, physical, and so on). With enough emotional intensity and repetition, our nervous systems experience something as real, even if it has not happened yet:

- *Failure forecasting:* Predicting that an idea will never work and putting little to no effort into the change

✏ *Self-fulfilling prophesies:* Repetitive failure forecasting, which eventually leads to performance problems, resignations or dismissals

Behavioral alignment is all about helping individuals process their world in a way that serves them versus alienating or destroying them. Behavioral Alignment seeks to reengineer individual belief systems and values to secure the customer's, the company's, and the employee's future.

Solution-driven breakthrough improvement must begin with a change in our fundamental beliefs. People need to associate pain with the status quo. If you are honest with yourself, you will recognize that pleasures have come about through change, growth, and new and empowering beliefs. The way people process change in their own minds has a big impact on results. The key to success is in reengineering individual abilities, capacities, and confidence (no one has deficient reengineering genes).

We have to modify people's belief systems so that they feel responsible for the outcomes of everything in their working and personal lives, whether they perform the work directly, support another area, provide information, or give advice to a team. This requires the following mind-set:

✏ Each employee is his or her own small-business, value-producing center

✏ The sum is a no-limit, fully functioning organization.

✏ Reengineering requires a totally different philosophy about work that is "children-like" and knows no limits.

Adjusting Belief Systems

During the past decade, we have sharpened our shop floor psychology skills by living through implementation after implementation with the people actually making change real. We have had the opportunity to work with thousands of people and have grown to appreciate their differences, feelings, emotions, and approaches to change. The reality of business and life is that, for one reason or another, everyone will not be performing at their full potential 100% of the time. We have developed a belief system hierarchy model, as shown in Figure 10.5, that helps individuals recognize what they are experiencing and how they can modify their beliefs to maximize individual and group performance.

There are five levels in the belief system hierarchy of adjustment:

1. Panic

    ✗ Going ballistic over a situation or outcome of an event (anger, anxiety)

    ✗ Absence of control is panic

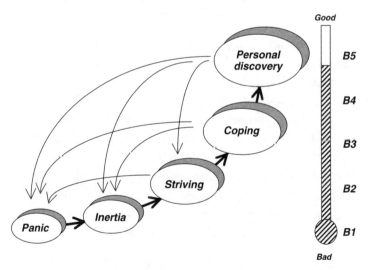

Figure 10.5 Belief System Hierarchy

✘ Aimless empowerment is worse than the absence of control

2. Inertia

✘ Being there without action, and hoping a situation will change without action

✘ Remain in the same motion (helplessness)

3. Striving

✘ Try the obvious and fail (defeat)

✘ Confirm "can't be done" (disappointment)

4. Coping

✘ Accept the "as is" and don't protest, make waves, or bug anyone (emotional ground swell)

5. Personal Discovery

✘ Hit the wall, refuse to live with situation

✘ Believe in a better way, "no limits"

✘ Never know failure (confidence, abilities) because you die trying!

People should strive to experience personal discovery because this is where they are at peak performance. What really happens is that people reach a peak and then trickle down to some lower level on the hierarchy. It is important to recognize where you are (B1, B2, B3) and why you arrived there, and then quickly initiate change internally to evolve upward in the belief system hierarchy.

The belief system hierarchy can be applied to group behavior as well to test the group's commitment to a particular purpose. The following list of potential observations can be matched closely to the belief system hierarchy:

✏ Denial, disbelief, inadequate, no change

✏ Interested, wait and see

- Believe in it, watch other's success
- Motivated, some participation
- Excited, regular participation
- Obsession, committed with heart, soul, emotions, passions, actions

Rapid breakthroughs are a function of the "obsessed critical mass," whether it is an individual, a VST, a portion of the company, or the entire organization.

Many companies have failed at their reenginnering, TQM, and other continuous improvement efforts because they failed to recognize the impact and importance of behavioral alignment on sustained performance. They have worked very hard at copying and shoehorning each other's improvement programs, but they have not really changed the way that people view their workplace on a day to day basis.

Figure 10.6 shows the migration of behavior in a change process. In the beginning of a change process, people are either enthusiastic beginners (BA1) or disillusioned experts (BA2). This area is critical because it determines the future rate of improvement and organizational learning, or if things will return to business as usual. Eventually, people develop into reluctant team players (BA3), where there is some level of improvement followed by a leveling off or a decline in performance. Relatively few organizations have evolved to the serious team player (BA4) level, because this type of performance really is indicative of reengineering, reinvention, constant paradigm shifts, and change as the norm.

The future-focused organization is made up of BA4 people. The organization is aligned because the behaviors and thinking processes of its individuals are aligned. Behavioral alignment is the foundation for charting and staying the course of revolutionary and continuous improvement.

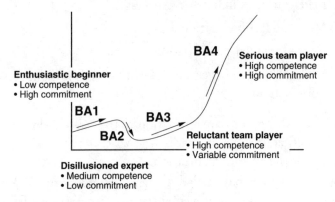

Figure 10.6   Behavioral Alignment

Summary

Throughout this book the focus has been on helping an organization and its leadership to develop a process to help answer the question of what to change to so that it will always be a viable force in its marketplace. The process described helps the organization to know what to change, how to cause the change in the most efficient and painless manner, and how to time and cause the change to happen. It knows what is important, what is a strength, what has value, and what does not. It knows when an approach has been useful and when to discard it. Its strategic business strategies now deal more with cultural change factors than traditional operational factors, since this will allow the organization to always be a viable force in its marketplace. The organization's leadership has learned to develop reliance on and trust in those in lateral and daily management positions since they have the fundamental understanding of the business. The leadership focuses on the panoramic future of the organization and leads by macromanagement and not the traditional micromanagement. Leadership focuses on those things that they can control, improve, or change.

The leadership has mastered the fine art of virtual partnerships interorganizational and external to the organization to maximize the leveraging of their scarce resources. They have common commitment at the top and alignment and partnerships throughout the rest of the organization to achieve their future-focused destiny.

The leadership has become masters of customized products and services, rapid response, assembling at the point of delivery globally, reducing overhead, inventory, and working capital, and constantly improving service standards.

The leadership expends their scarce resources to change how they service their customer base now and in the future and not on public relations to change their image. Their image is changed by their actions.

Organizations that follow this future-focused process will not be trying to duplicate past glory days[1] or to rejuvenate, renew, or reinvent themselves;[2] they are causing their competition to do this since they are the market pace setters for all others to imitate. These organizations are future-focused in all their actions. They do not wait for change to happen, but help make the change happen so that they have a degree of control that can be exploited for maximum gain.

A future-focused organization seeks to do the following:

- ✎ *Control its environment.* A future-focused organization is proactive in influencing emerging trends and possible governmental regulation. A future-focused organiza-

---

1. Can Xerox Duplicate Its Glory Days?, *Business Week*, October 4, 1993, No. 3339, pp. 56–58.
2. Why Mercedes Is Alabama Bound, *Business Week*, October 11, 1993, No. 3340, pp. 138–39.

tion is constantly monitoring its environment by using the tools and techniques introduced in this book. A future-focused organization is constantly on guard for any changes that will have an adversarial impact on the organization or marketplace. Understanding what is changing before it changes helps a future-focused organization's leadership to plan proactive intervention to shape an emerging trend into a positive business experience, while avoiding it having an adverse impact.

- *Control its marketplace and its competitors.* A future-focused organization is in the position to understand its customers' needs and expectations. It continually meets these needs and expectations since its customers view its product and services as value-added. It uses this approach to build consumer loyalty. A future-focused organization is always developing or improving its product or service line. It uses its R&D to funnel a continuous "seeds-to-needs" product or service development process. This seeds-to-needs approach helps a future-focused organization to influence or shape customer needs, as discussed in Chapter 6.

Following the above approach a future-focused organization sets up a deterrent to current or potential competitors from investing or competing in their marketplace. A Future Focused Organization is prepared to withstand a significant strategic competitive ploy because it is a flexible organization with the ability to change and redeploy resources quickly.

- *Control its destiny.* Becoming a future-focused organization is not an easy process because the organization has a history and legacy that may have unwanted baggage. Becoming a future-focused organization requires a substantial investment to overcome inappropriate capital, human, managerial, and physical decisions of the past. The decision to become a future-focused organization is one of deciding to control your destiny. A future-focused organization plots and monitors its progress and makes mid-course corrections to stay on course. This process requires a firm resolve on the part of the organization's management to invest in an organizational structure that can change rapidly and embrace changes as a way to fulfill its destiny.

In order for a future-focused organization to control its destiny it must do a superior job of making strategic decisions. Such decisions are made in a future-focused organization by listening to the marketplace and not to the executives' own ambitions. Strategic decisions in a future-focused organization are made after an in-depth assessment of the growth and profit potential, as well as the risk profile. The three components of the decision attributes, profit, growth, and risk, are compared to each other.

The comparison must be methodical and all potential trouble spots must be identified. Identified trouble spots must then be analyzed and detailed to determine if contingencies can be developed to overcome them or to reduce their impact. The Y-shaped matrix shown in Figure 11.1 is one analysis tool that could be used for this process. This type of analysis is the beginning of deciding on resource allocation priorities and guidelines.

In a future-focused organization, every day is a new beginning, with new opportunities and challenges. Every day is faced by a future-focused organization that is ready and capable to change. In a future-focused organization tradition is defined each day. Tradition is not an obstacle. Tradition does

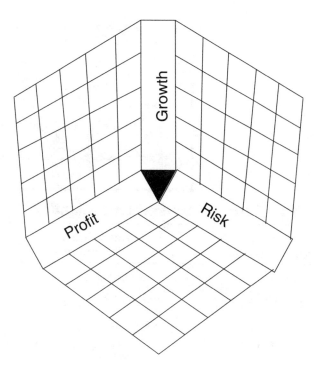

Figure 11.1   Y Analysis Matrix

not count in a future-focused organization as it does today in most organizations.

Closing Comments

A future-focused organization stops doing what comes naturally and reengineers its future. It is guided by the philosophy presented in Figure 11.2. Future-focused organizations influence and control their environment. They are a true seamless, learning organization that prosper and grow while their competition decays. Future-focused organizations set their sights high and are masters of boundaryless, out-of-the-box thinking.

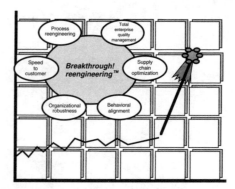

The Future-Focused Organization™

Stops Doing What Comes Naturally	Reengineers Its Future
Slow down, panic	Speed up, stay cool
Wait for instructions	Take the initiative
Get ready	Get going, *now!*
Try harder at more of the same	Shoot for the impossible, the absurd, the breakthrough
Try not to break things	Welcome controlled destruction, revolution
Avoid risks, mistakes	Welcome risk, mistakes
Benchmark other's success	Aim for perfection (0 ppm, 100%)
Be loyal to and improve the "as is"	Practice aloyalty, reinvention
Accept nature of business	Have faith in reengineering
Can't predict future	Define the future and make it happen
Act like an adult	Act like a child

Figure 11.2   The Guiding Philosophy

They recognize the differences between reengineering and rearranging. Future-focused organizations have discovered that the best way to predict the future is to invent it. They anticipate and change ahead of the times and not with it. Future-focused organizations view change and survival as synonymous, and they benefit from change and refuse outright to become victims of change.

Index

A

achieve, in culture, 78
acknowledgment, 51
affinity diagram process, 169
analyze in planning process, 172–74
assign in planning process, 172–74
attitude, 50–51
avoid, in culture, 78
awareness, 151

B

base-lining assessments, 166
behavioral alignment, 200–206
  belief systems adjustment in, 202–6
behaviors in communication process, 155–57
benefits, communication of, 156
betterment timeline, 124–25
BreakThrough Thinking, 105
business plan, integrated, 113

C

catalog companies, 139
catchball process, 110–13
change levers, 74
charting course, 193–206
check in planning process, 170
chosen thought in organization, 22–23
Chrysler Corporation, 44
collaboration, 51
colleges, 141
Commerce Department, U.S., 74
commitment, 51
communication process in virtual super team, 154–57
  behavior and outcome focus, 155–56
  benefits communication in, 156
  desired behaviors in, 157
  goal-setting and follow-up dates for, 157
  and listening for understanding, 156
  and self-esteem, 155

compensation views, 190
competitive analysis, 83–99
   evaluation, 88–98
      comparison summary, 98
      criteria comparisons, 93–97
      customer satisfaction anal-
         ysis, 92–93
      market scope, 90–91
      management in, 86–87
competitor's uniqueness, 135
concurrent engineering (CE), 89
concurrent exploration, 120
conscious speech, 23
consistent action, 23
constancy of purpose, 193, 195
constant care, 23
cooperation, 51
coping in belief systems adjustment, 204
criteria comparisons, 93–97
critical cultural factors, 118–19
critical cultural philosophies, 70
critical operational factors, 117–
   18
critical processes (CPs), 65–70
   attributes of, 66
critical purpose factors, 64–65,
   116
critical systems, 65–70
   attributes of, 66
   interaction, 70
culture, 57–58, 71–82
   analysis matrix, 75, 77
   change agents, 72–73
   climate checklist, 74–76
   critical factors, 118–19
   critical philosophies, 70
   cylinder, 73
   dimensions of, 81–82
   goals, 117
   interactions, 77
   potential plot, 79
   system, 71
   timeline, 124
customers, 25

analysis matrix, 135–37
expectations, 131–42
satisfaction analysis, 92–93
success function, 30–31

D

daily management, 34
   functions of, 127
decision-making in team standards, 163
Deming Prize, 44
Deming, W.E., 193
destiny control, 209–10
details in planning process, 172
dimensions
   of culture, 81–82
   of organization, 63
disillusioned experts (BA2), 205–
   6
Douglas Aircraft, 13

E

education, 151–52
educational institutions, 140–42
enthusiastic beginners (BA1),
   205–6
environmental control, 208
environmental scan process, 121–
   22
evaluation of personnel, 181–88
execution process, 25
explore in planning process, 168–
   69
external relationships, 84

F

failure forecasting, 201
filling stations, 137–38
financial approach, 110
Florida Power and Light, 13

force field analysis, 173
future change matrix, 125
future-focused organizations, 1–
        12
    characteristics of, 62–64
    cultural hierarchy in, 3–4
    and customer culture, 5–6
    guiding philosophy of, 212
    purpose hierarchy of, 3–4

G

Galileo Electro-Optics Corp., 24–
        27
Gantt chart, 175
generic vision statement process,
        107–8
goals
    in team standards, 163
    setting and follow-up dates in
        communication process,
        157
    statement form, 114

H

hardware stores, 138
high schools, 141
high-performance work teams,
        143
hiring and growing personnel,
        181
hiring, growing, rewarding pro-
        cess, 179–91
holistic, 152

I

inertia in belief systems adjust-
        ment, 204
information exchange in team
        standards, 162–63
insurance agents, 138–39

integrated teaming and planning
        model of virtual super
        team, 177
integration, 152
internal interrelationships, 84
International Quality Study, 102

J

joint accountability, 51

L

L-shaped matrix, 96
lateral management, 33–49
    characteristics of, 34–35
    creating, 39–41
    defining, 38–39
    developing, 41–42
    establishing, 42–43
    flow chart, 45–47
    rating plot, 53
    responsibility of, 36–37
leadership, 18–21, 207–8
    team standards of, 163–64
limited information collection,
        105
listening for understanding
        communication process, 156

M

management, 18, 21
    of business units, 120–24
    in competitive analysis pro-
        cess, 86–87
    types, 29
market
    domain, 134
    field location grid, 133
    percentage, 135
    potential, 135
    scope, 90–91

marketing field location tool,
    110
marketplace and competitor con-
    trol, 209
mission, vision, purpose (MVP)
    filtering, 7, 9

O

omni pattern, 57–82
omnicompetent phase in organi-
    zational patterns, 60
omnicomplacent phase in organi-
    zational patterns, 60–61
omnipotential phase in organiza-
    tional patterns, 69
omnislide phase in organization-
    al patterns, 61
operational business units
    (OBUs), 7–8
operational goals, 116
organization
    change levers, 74
    hierarchies, 69
    involvement, 13–27
    model, 133
    structure, 29–56
organizational robustness, 30,
    146, 149–53
ownership in organization, 18, 22

P

panic in belief systems, 203–4
participation, 152
patterns of growth and decline,
    59–62
    omnicompetent phase, 60
    omnicomplacent phase, 60–61
    omnipotential phase, 69
    omnislide phase, 61
people in organization, 58
permissiveness, 151

personal discovery in belief sys-
    tems, 204
personal growth form, 186, 187
personnel evaluation, 181–88
    proposal for new system, 184–
        88
philosophy, adopting new, 194
physical change levers, 74
pizza shops, 138
planning process, 101–30,
    165–75
    analyze and assign in, 172–74
    checking in, 170
    details of, 172
    exploring, 168–69
    and problem's magnitude,
        165–68
    sequence and track of, 175
    sorting and prioritizing of,
        169–70
    understanding of, 171–72
position description form, 184,
    185
position improvement form, 188,
    189
position selection summary form,
    181, 183
preserve, in culture, 78
prioritization matrix, 97
problem's magnitude in planning
    process, 165–68
processes in organizations, 58
product/service development ap-
    proach, 110
project selection criteria, 130
proposal for new system in per-
    sonnel evaluation, 184–
        88
psychological change levers, 74
purpose
    gap matrix, 196, 199
    hierarchy, 68
    of organization, 106–9
    plot, 196, 197

Q

quality function deployment
(QFD), 89

R

radar chart, 166–67
Rath and Strong, 14
rating plot in lateral management team, 53
regulations, 58
reluctant team players (BA3),
205–6
resources of team standards,
161–62
results management, 126–27
reward and compensation systems, 188–90
roles
in organizations, 16–17
in team standards, 161

S

savings and costs, 128–29
self-esteem in communication
process, 155
self-fulfilling prophesies, 202
sequence and track in planning
process, 175
serious team player (BA4), 205–6
silo syndrome, 143–45
SMART matrix, 119–21, 162, 174
solution-after-next, 124
sort and prioritize in planning
process, 169–70
status quo, 71–80
staying the course, 193–206
strategic future focus, 15–19
strategic management, 31–33
strategic planning model, 103–4
striving in belief systems, 204
suboptimization, 15

T

teams
and boundaryless skills, 148
and business skills, 148
and collaboration skills, 147
and consensus skills, 147
and constitution skills, 147,
149
and cooperation skills, 147
process of, 157–59
standards, 160–64
decision-making in, 163
goals in, 163
information exchange, 162–
63
leadership, 163–64
resources of, 161–62
roles in, 161
telephone companies, 139
total quality management
(TQM), 13–14, 24–27,
67, 139
transitional timeline, 122–23
tree diagram approach, 172–73
trust, 50, 52

U

understanding in planning process, 171–72
uniqueness range, 135
universal management, 151

V

values, 26
virtual super team (VST), 145–54
communication process in,
154–57
establishing, 159–60
integrated teaming and planning model in, 177
planning process in, 165–75

standards of, 160–64
  teaming process of, 157–59
visible symbols, 58

W

Wallace Company, 13
work teams, 143–77

Y

Y analysis matrix, 211